computers
    Ltd.

computers
Ltd.
what they *really* can't do

david harel

faculty of mathematics and computer science
the weizmann institute of science,
rehovot, israel

OXFORD
UNIVERSITY PRESS

OXFORD
UNIVERSITY PRESS

Great Clarendon Street, Oxford OX2 6DP

Oxford University Press is a department of the University of Oxford.
It furthers the University's objective of excellence in research, scholarship,
and education by publishing worldwide in

Oxford New York

Athens Auckland Bangkok Bogotá Buenos Aires Calcutta
Cape Town Chennai Dar es Salaam Delhi Florence Hong Kong Istanbul
Karachi Kuala Lumpur Madrid Melbourne Mexico City Mumbai
Nairobi Paris São Paulo Singapore Taipei Tokyo Toronto Warsaw

with associated companies in Berlin Ibadan

Oxford is a registered trade mark of Oxford University Press
in the UK and in certain other countries

Published in the United States by
Oxford University Press Inc., New York

British Library Cataloguing in Publication Data
Data available

Library of Congress Cataloguing in Publication Data
Harel, David, 1950–
computers Ltd.: what they really can't do/David Harel.
p. cm.
ISBN 0-19-850555-8
1.Computers. 2. Computer software. I. Title.

QA76.5. H3575 2000   004—dc21   00-023751

Typeset by EXPO Holdings, Malaysia
Printed in Great Britain by
Biddles Ltd, Guildford & King's Lynn

To Eynel
for so much more
than proposing the title

preamble

In 1984, *TIME* magazine ran a cover story on computer software. In the excellent article, the editor of a certain software magazine was quoted as saying:

> Put the right kind of software into a computer, and it will do whatever you want it to. There may be limits on what you can do with the machines themselves, but there are no limits on what you can do with software.

Wrong. Totally wrong. In fact, a simple way of summarizing this book is that it is devoted to describing and explaining the facts that refute — no, shatter! — this claim.

Of course, computers are incredible. They are without doubt the most important invention of the 20th century, having dramatically and irrevocably changed the way we live, and mostly for the better. But that is the good news, and good news is what most computer books are about. This book concentrates on the bad; on the negative side of things.

Computers are expensive, which is already bad news. They frustrate us: programming them is laborious and using them can be difficult; they are seductive, luring us away from more important things; they err; they crash; they contract viruses; and on and on. But it is not these kinds of bad news that concern us here. The goal of the book is to explain and illustrate one of the most important and fundamental facets of the world of computing — its inherent limitations.

Typically, when people have difficulties bending computers to their will, their excuses fall into three categories: insufficient money, insufficient time, and insufficient brains. Being richer, the argument goes, could buy us larger and more sophisticated computers, supported by better software; being younger or having a longer life-span would enable us to wait longer for time-consuming programs to terminate; and being smarter could lead to solutions that we don't seem able to find. These are strong and valid points, and we are not about to contest them: a more generous supply of any of these three commodities could indeed take us a long way. However, for the most part, our book is not about these kinds of hardships either. It concentrates on bad news that is *proven, lasting* and *robust*, concerning problems that computers are simply not able to solve, regardless of our hardware, software, talents or patience. And when we say 'proven', we mean really proven; that is, mathematically, and not just experimentally.

*   *   *

Why are we interested in bad news? Shouldn't computer scientists be spending their time making things smaller, faster, easier, more accessible and more powerful? Well, they should, and the vast majority of us actually do. But even so, starting in the 1930s, and increasingly so by the year, many researchers have been working hard to better understand the other side of the coin, that of humbling the computer, by discovering and better understanding its inherent weaknesses.

The motivation for this quest is four-fold:

- *To satisfy intellectual curiosity.* Just as physicists want to determine the ultimate confines of the universe or the constraints imposed by the laws of physics, so computer scientists want to discover what can be computed and what cannot, and how costly it is when it can.[1]

- *To discourage futile efforts.* Many people, among them knowledgeable computer experts, try to tackle computational problems that happen to be subject to devastating bad news. The more we understand these problems and their inherent nature, the less we shall waste our time and energy on such endeavors.

- *To encourage development of new paradigms.* Parallelism, randomization, heuristics, and quantum and molecular computing, five of the most promising and exciting topics in computer science research, would not be developing the way they are without the push resulting from the bad news.

- *To make possible the otherwise impossible.* To make possible the impossible?! This is surely paradoxical. How on earth can we hope to *profit* from bad news? Well, to keep up the suspense until Chapter 6, we shall only remark here that this is an unexpected aspect of our story, but also a surprisingly beneficial one.

So much for motivation. As to the nature of the bad news we discuss, consider the large body of very exciting work aimed at endowing computers with human-like intelligence. In its wake, a host of questions arise concerning the limits of computation, such

---

[1] To get a broad perspective on the kind of limitations scientists are interested in, see Barrow, J. D. (1998). *Impossibility: The Limits of Science and the Science of Limits.* Oxford University Press, Oxford.

as whether computers can run companies, carry out medical diagnosis, compose music or fall in love. While promising, and often quite amazing, progress has been made in addressing these issues (not very much on the last one, however), these questions are posed in an imprecise and vague manner. With the exception of the last chapter of the book, we avoid them. In contrast, we concentrate on precisely defined computational problems, that come complete with clear-cut objectives. This, in turn, makes it possible to make equally clear-cut statements about whether or not they can be solved satisfactorily.

The issues we discuss are not debatable, and do not involve philosophical, quasi-scientific arguments. Rather, we concentrate on hard facts, rigorously stated and mathematically proved. You don't go looking for triangles whose angles add up to 150° or 200° — although no-one has ever been able to inspect each and every triangle — simply because there is a proof that no such triangles exist.[2] In a similar way, if a computational problem has been proved to admit no solution, and we shall discuss such problems, then seeking a solution is pointless. The same goes for problems that do have solutions, but have been proved to require wholly unreasonably large computers (say, much larger than the entire known universe) or to take wholly unreasonable amounts of computation time (say, a lot more than has elapsed since the Big Bang), and we shall discuss many of these too.

* * *

---

[2] Planar ones, of course. On a spherical or almost spherical surface, such as the planet Earth, the sum of the angles of a triangle is in fact greater than 180°.

By and large, people are unaware of the issues this book addresses. Sadly and surprisingly, this is true also for many members of the computing profession itself, as the quote from *TIME* shows. This is really unfortunate. If the bad news were some esoteric, recently discovered phenomenon, not having come across it could be understood. The truth is that some parts of our story have been known for some 60 years, long before real computers were built, and most of the others have been steadily unfolding for the last 30.

To a large extent, the blame is on us — researchers in computer science. We have done far too little in exposing, exemplifying, illustrating, and making comprehensible the basics of our science in general, and its negative facets in particular. This leaves the public in general blissfully unstirred, free to follow with awe the technological advances in hardware and software, to delight in the excitement of new applications, and to gloat over the futuristic possibilities raised by instantaneous telecommunication, multi-media, virtual reality, artificial intelligence, and the global nature of the internet revolution.

There is no reason to break up the party. We should continue to strive for bigger and better things. But even so, a measure of humility is in place: computers are *not* omnipotent — far from it. Moreover, the problem is real, and it is here to stay.

acknowledgments

This book is based on the bad news parts of computer science, as exposed in my earlier book, *Algorithmics: The Spirit of Computing*, Addison-Wesley, 1987 (2nd edition, 1992). *Algorithmics* is not a popular science book. It is longer and a lot more technical than this one, and discusses the good news too. It was written for a technically oriented audience, and in its second edition it is also usable as a textbook. Some parts of the present book are indeed adapted from *Algorithmics*, but they are simplified and popularized, often quite significantly. I would like to thank Addison Wesley Longman for permission to use this material. Thanks also to *IEEE Spectrum* for permission to adapt R. W. Lucky's 'Jim's Phone' conversations in Chapter 7.

I am always extremely grateful to my home institution, The Weizmann Institute of Science in Israel, for providing the ideal supportive and encouraging environment for this kind of work. Thanks are due also to the Computer Science Department of Cornell University, Ithaca, NY, where I spent the academic year of 1994–1995; parts of the book were written there.

As in all my expository writing, it is a pleasure to acknowledge the influence of three colleagues, who are also researchers of the highest calibre, Amir Pnueli, Adi Shamir and Shimon Ullman.

In addition to the many people whose help is acknowledged in Algorithmics, I'd like to thank the following friends and colleagues for reading and commenting on parts of the manuscript, or for providing pointers and references: Dorit Aharonov, Liran Carmel, Judith Gal-Ezer, Stuart Haber, Lila Kari, Noam Nissan, Christos Papadimitriou, Ran Raz.

contents

chapter 1
what's it all about?

Computers are amazing. They seem to have it all. They fly aircraft and spaceships, and control power stations and hazardous chemical plants. Companies cannot be run without them, and many medical procedures cannot be performed in their absence. They serve lawyers and judges who seek judicial precedents, and help scientists and engineers to perform immensely involved mathematical computations. They route and control millions of simultaneous telephone calls and manage the remarkable movement of Internet data in enormous global networks. They execute tasks with great precision — from map-reading and typesetting to image processing, robot-aided manufacturing and integrated circuit design. They help individuals in many boring daily chores and at the same time provide entertainment through computer games or the delight of surfing the Web. Moreover, the computers of today are hard at work helping design the even more powerful computers of tomorrow.

It is all the more remarkable, therefore, that the digital computer — even the most modern and complex one — is merely a large collection of switches, called **bits,** each of which can be on or off. On is denoted by 1 and off by 0. Typically, the value of a bit is determined by some electronic characteristic, such as whether a certain point has a positive or negative charge. In a technical sense, a computer can really execute only a small number of extremely simple operations on bits, like flipping a bit's value, zeroing it, or testing it (that is, doing one thing if the bit is on and another if it is off).

Computers may differ in size, i.e. in the number of bits available, and in internal organization, as well as in the types of elementary operations allowed and the speed at which they are performed. They can also differ in outward appearance and in their connections with the external world. However, appearances are peripheral when compared to the bits and their internal arrangement. It is the bits that 'sense' the input stimuli arriving from the outside world, and it is the bits that 'decide' how to react to them by output stimuli. The inputs can arrive via keyboards, touch screens, control panels, electronic communication lines, or even microphones, cameras, and chemical sensors. The outputs are fed to the outside world via display screens, communication lines, printers, loudspeakers, beepers, robot arms, or whatever.

How do they do it? What is it that transforms simple operations like flipping zeros and ones into the incredible feats computers perform? The answer lies in the concepts that underlie the science of computing: the computational process, and the algorithm, or program, that causes it to take place.

algorithms

Imagine a kitchen, containing a supply of ingredients, an array of baking utensils, an oven, and a (human) baker. Baking is a process that *produces* a cake, *from* the ingredients, *by* the baker, *aided by* the oven, and, most significantly, *according to* the recipe. The ingredients are the **input** to the process, the cake is its **output**, and the recipe is the **algorithm**. In the world of electronic computation, the recipes, or algorithms, are embodied in **software**, whereas the utensils and oven represent the **hardware**. See Fig. 1.1.

Just like computers carrying out bit operations, the baker with his or her oven and utensils, has very limited direct abilities. This cake-baking hardware can pour, mix, spread, drip, knead, light the oven, open the oven door, measure time, measure quantities, etc. It cannot directly bake cakes. The recipes — those magical prescriptions that convert the limited abilities of novice bakers and kitchen hardware into cakes — are at the heart of the matter; not the ovens or the bakers.

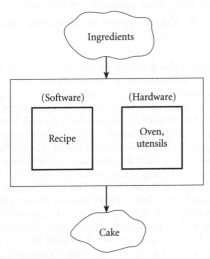

Fig. 1.1. Baking a cake.

In our world, recipes are called algorithms, and the study, knowledge, and expertise that concerns algorithms has been termed **algorithmics**.[1]

The analogy with cooking can be understood as follows: the recipe, which is an abstract entity, is the algorithm; the formal written version of the recipe, such as is found in a particular cookbook, is analogous to a **computer program** — the precise representation of an algorithm, written in a special computer-readable formalism called a **programming language**. It is important to realize that, just as a recipe remains the same whether written in English, French, or Latin, and regardless of where and by whom it is carried out, so does an algorithm remain the same whether written in Fortran, C, Cobol, or Java, and regardless of the computer it runs on, be it an ultra-light laptop or a room-size mainframe. The generic term **software** actually refers to programs rather than to the abstract notion of algorithms, since software is

---

[1] The word 'algorithm' is derived from the name of the Arabic/Persian mathematician of the ninth century, Mohammed al-Khowârizmî, who is credited with providing the step-by-step rules for carrying out the fundamental operations of decimal arithmetic. In Latin the name became Algorismus, from which 'algorithm' is derived. Historically, the first nontrivial algorithm was invented somewhere between 400 and 300 BC by the great Greek mathematician Euclid. The **Euclidian algorithm**, as it is called, finds the greatest common divisor (gcd) of two positive integers, i.e. the largest integer that exactly divides them both. For example, the gcd of 80 and 32 is 16. The word 'algorithmics' was apparently coined by J. F. Traub (1964). *Iterative Methods for the Solution of Equations*, Prentice Hall. It was proposed as the name for the relevant field of study by D. E. Knuth (1985). 'Algorithmic Thinking and Mathematical Thinking', *American Math. Monthly* 92, 170–181, and by the present author in *Algorithmics: The Spirit of Computing*, Addison-Wesley (1987).

written for real computers. However, we shall blur the distinction, since the story told in the following chapters applies just as well to both.

basic instructions

Let us take the gastronomical analogy a little further. Here is a recipe for chocolate mousse.[2] The ingredients — that is, the recipe's input — include 8 ounces of semi-sweet chocolate pieces, 2 tablespoons of water, a 1/4 cup of powdered sugar, 6 separated eggs, and so on. The output is described as six to eight servings of delicious *mousseline au chocolat*:

> Melt chocolate and 2 tablespoons water in double boiler. When melted, stir in powdered sugar; add butter bit by bit. Set aside. Beat egg yolks until thick and lemon-colored, about 5 minutes. Gently fold in chocolate. Reheat slightly to melt chocolate, if necessary. Stir in rum and vanilla. Beat egg whites until foamy. Beat in 2 tablespoons sugar; beat until stiff peaks form. Gently fold whites into chocolate-yolk mixture. Pour into individual serving dishes. Chill at least 4 hours. Serve with whipped cream, if desired. Makes 6 to 8 servings.

This is the 'software' relevant to the preparation of the mousse; it is the algorithm that prescribes the process that produces mousse from the ingredients. The process itself is carried out by the person preparing the mousse, together with the 'hardware', in this case the various utensils: double boiler, heating apparatus, beater, spoons, timer, and so on.

---

[2] From Sinclair and Malinowski (1978). *French Cooking*. Weathervane Books, p. 73.

One of the basic instructions, or basic actions, present in this recipe is '*stir in powdered sugar*'. Why does the recipe not say '*take a little powdered sugar, pour it into the melted chocolate, stir it in, take a little more, pour, stir,...*'? Even more specifically, why does it not say '*take 2,365 grains of powdered sugar, pour them into the melted chocolate, pick up a spoon and use circular movements to stir it in,...*'? Or, to be even more precise, why not '*move your arm towards the ingredients at an angle of 14°, at an approximate velocity of 18 inches per second,...*'? The answer, of course, is obvious. The 'hardware' knows how to stir powdered sugar into melted chocolate, and does not need further details.

This begs the question of whether the hardware knows how to prepare sugared and buttered chocolate mixture, in which case the entire first part of the recipe could be replaced by the simple instruction '*prepare chocolate mixture*'. Taking this to the extreme, perhaps the hardware knows how to do the whole thing. This would make it possible to replace the entire recipe by '*prepare chocolate mousse*', indeed a perfect recipe for producing the chocolate mousse; it is clear and precise, contains no mistakes, and is guaranteed to produce the desired output just as required.

Obviously, the level of detail is very important when it comes to an algorithm's elementary instructions. The actions that the algorithm asks to be carried out must be tailored to fit the capabilities of the hardware that does this carrying out. Moreover, the actions should also match the comprehension level of a human. This is because humans construct algorithms, humans must become convinced that they operate correctly, and humans are the ones who maintain those algorithms and possibly modify them for future use.

Consider another example, which is closer to conventional computation: multiplying integers manually. Suppose we are asked to multiply 528 by 46. The usual 'recipe' for this is to first multiply the 8 by the 6, yielding 48, to write down the units digit of the result, 8, and to remember the tens digit, 4. The 2 is then multiplied by the 6, and the 4 is added, yielding 16. The units digit 6 is then written down to the left of the 8 and the tens digit 1 is remembered. And so on.

The same questions can be asked here too. Why '*multiply the 8 by the 6*'? Why not '*look up the entry appearing in the eighth row and sixth column of a multiplication table*', or '*add 6 to itself 8 times*'? Similarly, why can't we solve the entire problem in one stroke by the simple and satisfactory algorithm '*multiply 528 by 46*'? This last question is rather subtle: we are allowed to multiply 8 by 6 directly, but not 528 by 46. Why?

Again, the level of detail plays a crucial part in our acceptance of the multiplication algorithm. We assume that the relevant hardware (in this case, ourselves) is capable of carrying out 8 times 6 directly, but not 528 times 46, so that the former can be used as a basic instruction in an algorithm for carrying out the latter.

Another point illustrated by these examples is that different problems are naturally associated with different kinds of basic actions. Recipes entail stirring, mixing, pouring, and heating; multiplying numbers entails addition, digit multiplication, and remembering a digit; looking up a telephone number might entail turning a page, moving a finger down a list, and comparing a given name to the one being pointed out. Interestingly, we shall see later that when it comes to algorithms intended for computers these differences are inessential.

the text vs. the process

Suppose we are given a list of personnel records, one for each employee in the company. Each record contains an employee's name, some other details, and his or her salary. We are interested in the total sum of the salaries of all employees. Here is an algorithm for this:

1. make a note of the number 0;

2. proceed through the list, adding the current employee's salary to the noted number;

3. having reached the end of the list, produce the noted number as output.

Clearly, the algorithm does the job. The 'noted' number can be thought of as a sort of empty box containing a single number, whose value can change. Such an object is often called a **variable**. In our case, the noted number starts out with the value zero. After the addition in line 2 is carried out for the first employee, its value is that employee's salary. After the addition for the second employee, its value is the sum of the salaries of the first two employees, and so on. At the end, the value of the noted number is the sum of all salaries (see Fig. 1.2).

It is interesting that the *text* of this algorithm is short and is fixed in length, but the *process* it describes varies with the size of the employee list, and can be very, very long. Two companies, the first with 10 employees and the second with a million, can both use the very same algorithm to sum their respective employees' salaries. The process, though, will be much faster for the first company than for the second. Moreover, not only is the text of the algorithm short and of fixed size, but both companies require only a single variable (the noted number) to do the job. So the quantity of 'utensils' is also small and fixed. Of course, the *value* of the noted number will be larger for a larger company, but only a single number is required to be 'noted' all along.

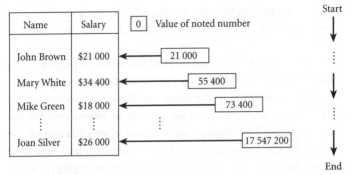

Fig. 1.2. Summing salaries.

Thus we have a fixed algorithm, that requires no change in order to be used in different situations (i.e. for each and every different input list), but the processes it prescribes can differ in length and duration for different input situations.

inputs

Even the simple example of salary summation shows a variety of possible inputs: small companies, large companies, companies in which some salaries are zero, or ones in which all salaries are equal. The algorithm might also have to deal with unusual or even bizarre inputs, such as companies with no employees at all or with employees who receive negative salaries (that is, the employee pays the company for the pleasure of working for it).

Actually, the salary algorithm is supposed to perform satisfactorily for an *infinite* number of perfectly acceptable lists of employees. This is an extreme way of appreciating the 'short-algorithm-for-lengthy-process' principle. Not only the contrast in duration, or length, is interesting; the very *number* of processes prescribed by a single algorithm of fixed length can be large, and most often is infinite.[3]

An algorithm's inputs must be **legal** relative to its purpose. This means that the *New York Times* list of bestsellers would be unacceptable as an input to the salary summation algorithm, just as peanut butter and jelly are unacceptable as ingredients for the mousse recipe. This means that we need a **specification** of the allowed inputs. Someone must decide precisely which employee lists are legal and which ones are not, where an employee record ends and another begins, where exactly in each record the salary is to be found and whether it is given in longhand (for example, $32 000) or in some abbreviated form (e.g. $32K), and so on.

what do algorithms solve?

All this leads us to the central notion underlying the world of algorithmics and computation — the **algorithmic problem**, which is what an algorithm is designed to solve. The description of an algorithmic problem must include two items (see Fig. 1.3):

- a precise definition of the set of legal inputs;
- a precise characterization of the required output as a function of the input.

---

[3] This issue of an infinite number of potential inputs doesn't quite fit the recipe analogy, since although a recipe should work perfectly well no matter how many times it is used, ingredients are usually described in fixed quantities. Hence, the recipe really has only one potential input. However, the chocolate mousse recipe could have been made generic, to fit varying but proportional quantities of ingredients.

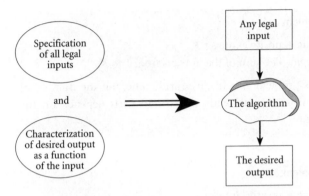

The algorithmic problem   An algorithm solving the problem

Fig. 1.3. The algorithmic problem and its solution.

When we discuss an algorithmic problem as applied to a particular
input (like the salary summation problem applied to some con-
crete list of employees), we call it an **instance** of the problem.

Here now are some additional examples of algorithmic problems. Each one is defined, as is proper, by its set of legal inputs
and a description of the desired output. They are numbered,
and we will refer to them at various points in the following
chapters.

Problem 1

Input: Two integers, J and K.
Output: The number $J^2 + 3K$.

This is a simple problem that calls for an arithmetic calculation on two input numbers.

Problem 2

Input: A positive integer K.
Output: The sum of the integers from 1 to K.

This problem also involves arithmetic, but the number of elements it deals with varies, and itself depends on the input.

Problem 3

Input: A positive integer K.
Output: 'Yes' if K is prime and 'No' if it isn't.

This is what we shall be referring to as a decision problem. It calls for deciding the status of its input number. (Recall that a **prime number** is a positive integer that can be divided without a remainder only by 1 and itself. For example, 2, 17, and 113 are primes, whereas 6, 91, and 133 are not. Non-primes are termed **composite**.) Solving this problem will surely involve arithmetic, but it does not provide a numeric output, only a 'Yes' or a 'No'.

Problem 4

Input: A list L of words in English.
Output: The list L sorted in alphabetic (lexicographic) order.

This is a non-arithmetical problem, but like Problem 2 it has to deal with a varying number of elements; in this case words.

Problem 5

Input: Two texts in English.
Output: A list of the words common to the two texts.

This too involves words, rather than numbers. We assume that texts have been defined appropriately, say, as a string of symbols consisting of letters, spaces and punctuation marks. A word in a text would be a string of letters enclosed by spaces or punctuation marks.

Problem 6

Input: A road map of cities with distances attached to road segments, and two designated cities therein, A and B.
Output: A description of the shortest possible path (trip) between A and B.

This is a search problem, involving points and distances between them. It calls for some kind of optimization process to find the shortest path.

Problem 7

Input: A road map of cities, with distances attached to road segments, and a number K.
Output: 'Yes' if it is possible to take a trip that passes through all the cities, and whose total length is no greater than K miles, and 'No' if such a trip is impossible.

This too asks to search for a short path, not between two points but, rather, a path that traverses *all* points. Also, this problem is not phrased as requiring an optimization (i.e. find the 'best' path), but as a decision problem that asks just whether there is some path shorter than the given limit.

Problem 8

Input: A program P written in Java, with integer input variable X and output variable Y, and a number K.
Output: The number $2K$ if the program P always sets Y's value to be equal to X^2, and $3K$ if not.

This problem is about algorithms, in their formal attire as programs. It wants to know something about the behavior of a given program in general; not of a particular input.

So algorithmic problems have all kinds of inputs: numbers, words, texts, maps, and even other algorithms or programs. Also, some problems are truly computational in nature, some involve rearrangements (sorting), some require information retrieval (finding common words), some are optimization problems (shortest path), and some are decision problems (primality testing and all-point trips). Thus, a **decision problem** is a yes/no algorithmic problem. Decision problems appear not to compute, retrieve or optimize, only to *decide*, determining whether some property is true or false. Some algorithmic problems are hybrids: Problem 8, for example, combines decision with computation; its output is the result of one of two simple computations, but which of these it will be depends on a property of the input that has to be decided.

All these sample problems have infinite sets of legal inputs. To solve them, we have to be able to deal with arithmetic on *all* numbers, with sorting *all* lists of words, with finding the shortest trip in *all* city maps, etc. Put another way, each problem requires that we devise a method, a common procedure or recipe, that will solve *any* given instance of the problem. The number of potential instances is infinite. Such a method constitutes an algorithm.

Many algorithmic problems in the real everyday world are not so easy to define. Sometimes the difficulty is in specifying the required output, as when asking for the best move from a legal board position in chess (what exactly is 'best'?). In other cases, describing the inputs can be complicated. Suppose 20 000 newspapers are to be distributed to 1000 delivery points in 100 towns using 50 trucks. The input contains the road distances between the towns and between the delivery points in each town, the number of newspapers required at each point, the present location of each truck, details of available drivers, including their present whereabouts, and each truck's newspaper carrying ability, gasoline capacity and miles-per-gallon performance. The output is to be a list, matching drivers and destinations to trucks, in a way that minimizes the total cost to the distributing company. Actually, the problem calls for an algorithm that works for any number of newspapers, towns, delivery points, and trucks.

Some problems have hard-to-pin-down inputs as well as hard-to-specify outputs, such as the ones required to predict the weather or to evaluate stock market investments.

In this book, we shall stick to simple-looking algorithmic problems, usually with easy to describe inputs and outputs. In fact, for the most part, we will concentrate on decision problems. So describing our problems will be easy, and the outputs will usually be just 'Yes's and 'No's.

isn't our setup too simplistic?

Aren't we overly simplifying things? Computers are busy struggling with tasks far more complicated than merely reading a simple input, doing some work, producing a 'Yes' or a 'No' and quitting. Aren't we greatly weakening our presentation by avoiding modern real-world computational frameworks, such as interactive computing, distributed systems, real-time embedded systems, graphics-intensive applications, multimedia, and the entire world of the Internet?

To me, the author, you might be saying under your breath 'Are you just another one of those stuffy academics? Don't you know *anything* about computing? Stop giving us this chit-chat about simple input/work/output computations. Just get real, will you?'.

The answer is: indeed, yes. We *are* simplifying things, and in fact quite radically. But for a very good reason. Remember that we are dealing with the *bad* news. This book is not about making things better, smaller, stronger, or faster. It is about showing that very often things *cannot* be improved in these ways. That things can become very, very nasty. That certain tasks are simply impossible. Now, given that we are after bad news here, our arguments and claims become *stronger*, not weaker, by considering a simpler class of problems! We will be showing that even in a simple computational framework things can be devastatingly bad; all the more so in an intricate and seemingly more powerful one. The fact that computers are hopelessly limited is *more* striking with a simple input–output paradigm for computation than with a more complex one. Moreover, since the book is devoted almost exclusively to decision problems, we are also implying that the bad news has nothing to do with the need for complicated and lengthy outputs. The desire to generate even a simple 'Yes' or 'No' is enough to yield real nightmares.

solving algorithmic problems

An algorithmic problem is **solved** when an appropriate algorithm has been found. What is 'appropriate'? Well, the algorithm must provide correct outputs for all legal inputs: if the algorithm is **exe-**

cuted, or run, on any one of the legal inputs defined in the problem, it must produce the output specified in the problem for that input. A solution algorithm that works well for *some* of the inputs is not good enough.

Finding solutions to most of the sample problems described earlier is easy. Computing $J^2 + 3K$ is trivial (assuming, of course, that we have basic operations for addition and multiplication), and likewise summing the integers from 1 to K. In the latter case, of course, we must use a **counter** to keep track of how far we have gone and to stop the process when we have dealt with K itself.

To test whether a number K is prime (Problem 3), we divide it by all the integers from 2 to $K - 1$, stopping and saying 'No' if one of them is found to divide K without a remainder, and stopping and saying 'Yes' only when all the divisions have been completed and they have all yielded a remainder.[4]

Problem 4 can be solved by numerous different sorting algorithms. A simple one involves repeatedly searching for the smallest element in the input list L, removing it from L and adding it to the accumulating output list. The process stops when the original list is empty. Problems 6 and 7 can both be solved by considering all possible paths between cities (that is, one-way paths between A

---

[4] Of course, this algorithm can be improved: we can stop the process of testing for divisors at $\sqrt{K}$, the square root of K, rather than at $K - 1$. The reason is that if K has a clean divisor that is larger than $\sqrt{K}$ it must also have one that is smaller. We can also avoid testing multiples of the numbers already tested, thus further expediting the process. Some of the other problems can also be solved more efficiently than the ways we mention. However, efficiency and practicality of algorithms are not addressed until later in the book, so we shall not dwell on these issues right now. Here we impose only the minimal requirement — that the algorithm does, in fact, solve the problem, providing correct outputs for all legal inputs, even though it might do so inefficiently.

and B in Problem 6, and round-trip paths that traverse all the cities in Problem 7), and computing their lengths. Since the number of cities is finite, the number of paths is finite too, so that an algorithm can be set up to run through them all. This has to be done with care, however, so as not to miss any paths, and not to consider paths more times than is needed.

As mentioned, we shall return to several of these sample problems in the following chapters.

programming

An important issue that we should address, although it is not really critical to the central concerns of the book, is the way algorithms are executed by real computers. How do computers bridge the gap between their extremely modest capability to carry out operations on bits and the high-level actions humans use to describe algorithms? For example, how can bit manipulation be made to accomplish even such a simple-looking task as '*proceed through the list, adding the current employee's salary to the noted number*'? What list? Where does the computer find the list? How does it proceed through the list? Where exactly is the salary to be found? How is the 'noted number' accessed? And so on.

We have already mentioned that algorithms must be presented to the computer in a rigorous, unambiguous fashion, since when it comes to precision and unambiguity, '*proceed through the list*' is not much better than '*beat egg whites until foamy*'. This rigor is achieved by presenting the computer with a **program**, which is a carefully formulated version of the algorithm, suitable for computer execution. It is written in a **programming language**, which provides the notation and rules by which one writes programs for the computer.

A programming language must have a rigid **syntax**, allowing the use of only special words and symbols. Any attempt to stretch this syntax might turn out to be disastrous. For example, if '**input** K' is written in a language whose input commands are of the form '**read** K', chances are that the result will be something like 'SYNTAX ERROR E4514 IN LINE 108'. And of course, we cannot hope to address the computer with the like of '*please read a value for K from the input*', or '*how about getting me a value for K*'. These might result in a long string of obscure error messages. It is true that nice, talkative instructions, such as the ones we find in recipes, are more pleasant and perhaps less ambiguous than their terse and impersonal equivalents. It is also true that we strive to make computers as user-friendly as possible. But since we are still far from computers that can understand free-flowing natural language like English (see Chapter 7), a formal, concise, and rigid set of syntactic rules is essential.

An algorithm for summing the numbers from 1 to K might be written in a typical programming language as follows:

```
input K
X: = 0
for Y from 1 to K do
    X: = X + Y
end
output X
```

The intended meaning of this program is as follows. First, K is received as an input and the variable X (a 'noted number') is assigned an initial value of zero. Its role will be to accumulate the running sum we are calculating. Next, a **loop** is carried out, calling for its **body** — in our case the $X: = X + Y$ that appears between the

for command and the **end** — to be executed again and again. The loop is controlled by the variable Y, which starts out with the value 1 and increases repeatedly by 1 until it reaches K, which is the last time the $X := X + Y$ is executed. This causes the computer to consider all the integers from 1 to K, in that order, and in each iteration through the loop the integer considered is added to the current value of X. In this way X accumulates the required sum. When the loop is completed, the final sum is output.

Of course, this is what we *intend* the program to mean, which is not enough. The computer must somehow be told about the intended meaning of programs. This is done by a carefully devised **semantics** that assigns an unambiguous meaning to each syntactically allowed phrase in the programming language. Without this, the syntax is worthless. If meanings for instructions in the language have not been provided and somehow 'explained' to the computer, the program segment 'for Y from 1 to K do' might, for all we know, mean 'subtract Y from 1 and store the result in K', instead of it being the controlling command of the loop, as we intended. Worse still, who says that the keywords **from, to, do**, for example, have anything at all to do with their meaning in English? Maybe the very same program segment means 'erase the computer's entire memory, change the values of all variables to zero, output "TO HELL WITH PROGRAMMING LANGUAGES", and stop!'. Who says that ': =' stands for 'assign to', and that '+' denotes addition? And on and on. We might be able to *guess* what is meant, since the language designer probably chose keywords and special symbols intending their meaning to be similar to some accepted norm. But a computer cannot be made to act on such assumptions.

To summarize, a programming language comes complete with rigid rules that prescribe the allowed *form* of a legal program, and also with rules, just as rigid, that prescribe its *meaning*. We can now phrase, or **code** our algorithms in the language, and they will be unambiguous not only to a human observer, but to the computer too.

Once the program is read in by the computer, it undergoes a number of computerized transformations, aimed at bringing it down to the bit-manipulation level that the computer really 'understands'. At this point the program (or, rather, its low-level equivalent) can be run, or executed, on a given input (see Fig. 1.4).[5]

errors and correctness

Coming up with a bright idea for an algorithm, constructing the algorithm itself carefully and then writing it up formally as a program, doesn't mean we are done. Consider the following:

- Several years ago, around her 107th birthday, an elderly lady received a computerized letter from the local school authorities in a Danish county, with registration forms for first grade in elementary school. It turned out that only two digits were allotted to the 'age' field in the population database.

- In January 1990, one of AT&T's switching systems in New York City failed, causing a major crash of the national AT&T telephone system. For nine hours, almost half of the calls made through AT&T failed to connect. As a result, the company lost

---

[5] The main transformation among these is called **compilation**. The **compiler**, which is itself a piece of software, transforms the high-level program into a functionally equivalent program written in a low-level format called **assembly language**, which is much closer to the **machine language** of bit manipulation.

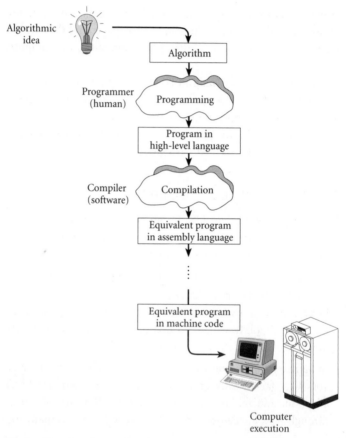

Fig. 1.4. Transforming an algorithm into machine code.

more than \$60 million, not to mention the enormous losses accrued by airlines, hotels, banks, and all kinds of other establishments that rely critically on the telephone network. The failure was caused by a software flaw, and escaped detection even by the complex software-testing methods of AT&T. Moreover, although the error was in a single program, it caused a cascade of failures that avalanched through the entire system, resulting in what turned out to be essentially a collapse of the entire network.

- In June 1996, less than a minute into its first flight, the French rocket Ariane 5 self-destructed, causing direct and indirect losses of several billions of dollars, and many months of setback for the entire Ariane space program. In the words of the inquiry board, the failure was caused by 'the complete loss of guidance and attitude information 37 seconds after start of the main engine ignition sequence', and that this was 'due to specification and design errors in the software of the inertial reference system'. The error, it turned out, was in a single line of code that attempted to load a 64-bit number into a 16-bit location in the computer, causing overflow.

These are just three of numerous tales of software failures, many of which have ended in catastrophes, at times with loss of life. It is naïve to assume that the algorithms and programs we write will always do exactly what we had in mind. Getting them to be correct takes lots and lots of very hard work, and is often unsuccessful.

The correctness issue has surfaced recently in all its severity around the so called **Y2K problem**, or the 2000 year bug, which is expected to come to a climax at the turn of the century, when computers that used two digits for storing years will have to start dealing with dates that have a year component of 00 or 05. At the time of writing (mid-1999) no-one knows the extent of the difficulties or catastrophes this will cause; immense efforts and enormous amounts of money have been put into minizing its impact.[6] Put very simply, definitions of algorithmic problems in the past did not normally take into account years that go beyond 1999.

Footnote 6 can be found on p. 24

Establishing correctness is particularly difficult because algorithms are required to produce the right outputs when run on any
one of the legal inputs specified in the problem. Partial solutions
are unacceptable. To use the example of testing a number for primality (Problem 3), it would be laughable if someone were to pro-
pose an algorithm that works well for half of the inputs — the even
numbers.[7] As a more extreme example, consider the following
trivial algorithm for summing salaries:

1. produce 0 as output.

This 'algorithm' works perfectly well for several interesting lists of
employees: those with no employees at all, those in which everyone
earns $0.00, or those with a payroll that reflects a perfect balance
between positive and negative salaries. Clearly, this is not good
enough. Our algorithms have to work as required for *all* legal
inputs. This is a strict requirement: we want complete, foolproof
solutions. No almosts. (In Chapter 6 we shall relax this somewhat,
but for now these are the rules of the game.)

A frequent kind of error stems from abusing the syntax of the
programming language. If we write 'read X' when the programming language requires '**input** X', or even merely misspell the word
input, there is no way for the computer to know what we meant,
and the program will not be able to run or will produce garbage. So
we must be careful with that. Nevertheless, syntax errors are but a
troublesome manifestation of the fact that algorithms run by com-

---

[6] Added in proof-reading (early 2000): fortunately, the morning of
January 1, 2000 went by without too much trouble. Curiously, instead of
applauding, and being grateful for all this work, some people have tried
to claim that the whole issue was a hoax to begin with.

[7] The only even prime is 2.

puter are required to be presented in formal attire.[8] Much worse are **logical errors**. These do not mean that something is wrong with the program as is, but simply that it doesn't solve the algorithmic problem we had in mind. Unlike syntax errors, logical errors can be notoriously elusive. They often reflect flaws in the very design of the algorithm. Someone once said that logical errors are like mermaids — the fact that you haven't seen one doesn't mean they don't exist.[9]

The quest to eliminate logical errors in algorithmics is a deep and complex topic, and is outside the scope of this book. The naïve method is to repeatedly execute the program on many different test inputs, checking the results. This process is called **debugging**, a name with an interesting history: one of the early computers stopped working one day and was found to have a large insect jammed in a crucial part of its circuitry. Since then, errors, usually logical errors, are affectionately termed **bugs**.

All this has to do with the algorithms and programs — the software. As far as hardware goes, computers make less mistakes. A hardware error is quite a rarity these days, despite the famed 1997 bug in Intel's Pentium II chip. In fact, when our bank statement is in error and we are told that the computer made a mistake, it was most certainly not the computer that erred but one of the humans involved in the bank's computerization process. Either incorrect data was input to the program, or the program itself, written, of course, by a human, contained an error.

---

[8] Many compilers are made to spot syntax errors, and will notify the programmer, who will typically be able to correct them with little effort.

[9] See G. D. Bergland (1981). 'A Guided Tour of Program Design Methodologies', *Computer* **14**, 13–37.

termination

An algorithm that completes its work but produces the wrong output is just one kind of worry. When it comes to the need for our algorithms and programs to do what we expect, there is something else we have to worry about — an algorithm that doesn't terminate at all, but, rather, keeps running on its input forever. This is clearly an error too. We don't want our programs to loop forever, i.e. to get stuck in an infinite non-terminating computation. The execution of a program on any one of its legal inputs should terminate within a finite amount of time, and its output must be the correct one.

Often, we can see rather easily how to make sure that our algorithm terminates. As a simple example, suppose we are devising an algorithm to check the primality of a number. We might have decided, rather stupidly, to base our approach directly on the definition of a prime number, verbatim. That is, in an attempt to find a factor (a divider) of the input number, we instruct our algorithm to try to divide it by each and every number from 2 on, in turn, with no bounds set. This rather silly algorithm would clearly loop indefinitely when run on a number that was indeed prime. Fortunately, as we have seen, there are obvious ways to bound the number of candidate divisors that need to be tested, and these guarantee termination.

Contrast this example with Problem 8 of the list given earlier, in which we don't seem to be that lucky: a solution algorithm is required to give one answer if the input program P behaves in some particular way, and another answer if it doesn't. There appears to be no way for us to make the decision without actually *running P*, a process that can itself fail to terminate. Worse, it seems that we have to run P on infinitely many inputs, not just on one or two.

We shall return to this example in the next chapter.

chapter 2

sometimes we can't do it

The message of this chapter is simple and clear. Computers are not omnipotent. They can't do everything. Far from it.

We shall discuss problems that cannot be solved by *any* computer, past, present or future, running *any* program that can be devised, even if given unlimited amounts of time and even if endowed with unlimited storage space and other resources it might need. We still require, of course, that algorithms and programs terminate for each legal input in a finite amount of time, but we allow that time to be unlimited. The algorithm can take as long as it wishes, and can use whatever resources it asks for in the process, but it must eventually stop and produce the right output. Nevertheless, even under these generous conditions, we shall see interesting and important problems for which there simply are no algorithms, and it doesn't matter how smart we are, or how sophisticated and powerful our computers, our software, our programming languages and our algorithmic methods. Figure 2.1 is intended to set the stage for what is to come.

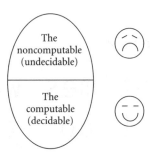

Fig. 2.1. The sphere of algorithmic problems: Version I.

These facts have deep philosophical implications, not only on the limits of machines like computers, but also on our own limits as beings with finite mass. Even if we were given unlimited amounts of pencil and paper, and an unlimited lifespan, there would be well-defined problems we could not solve. It is also important to stress that this is not just a fact about computing, by brain or by machine. It is a fact about *knowing*. In a strong sense, what we can compute is what we are able to figure out by careful step-by-step processes from what we already know. The limits of computation are the limits of knowledge. We may have insight and depth, and some people have astonishing brilliance, but there is a strong case to the effect that what is deducible from facts is what can be computed from them algorithmically.

Some people are opposed to drawing such sweeping conclusions from mere algorithmic results, and indeed we shall not get into this more general issue. It definitely deserves a broader treatment. Instead, we shall stick to the mathematically rigorous aspects of pure algorithmics, leaving the speculative and controversial facets of our story to philosophers and cognitive scientists.

finite problems are solvable

The first thing to notice is that any algorithmic problem with a finite set of inputs is solvable. That is, if all it will ever have to deal with is a finite, limited set of possible inputs, there is an algorithm to solve it. Suppose we have a decision problem whose sole legal inputs are the items *input*1, *input*2, … , *inputK*. Then there is an algorithm that 'contains' a table providing each of the *K* inputs with the appropriate output. It might look like this:

1.   read the input;

2.   if it is *input*1 then output 'Yes' and stop;

3.   if it is *input*2 then output 'Yes' and stop;

4.   if it is *input*3 then output 'No' and stop;

…

…

K + 1. if it is *inputK* then output 'Yes' and stop.

This works, of course, because it is possible to 'hard-wire' into an algorithm the entire algorithmic problem in all its glory by tabulating all the (finitely many) input–output pairs. It might be difficult to figure out the tabulation itself, that is, to *construct* such a table-driven algorithm, but we are not interested in this meta-difficulty here. For the present discussion, it suffices to know that for finitary problems solutions exist, and we ignore the issue of how to find them.

In contrast, algorithmic problems that have *infinite* sets of legal inputs are the really interesting ones. For these, we don't even know if there *exists* a finite algorithm to tackle the infinitely many different cases, and it is those that will keep us busy.

the tiling problem

Our first example of a noncomputable problem involves covering large areas using colored tiles. A **tile** is defined to be 1×1 square, divided into four by the diagonals, each quarter colored with some color. We assume that the tiles have fixed orientation and cannot be rotated.[1]

An input is a finite number of tile descriptions, collectively denoted by T. Each tile type in T is defined by its four colors in order. The problem asks whether any finite area, of any size (with integer dimensions, of course), can be covered using only tiles of the kinds described in T, but adhering to the following restriction: the colors on the touching edges of any two adjacent tiles must be identical. An unlimited number of tiles of each type is available, but in T there is only a finite, limited number of *types* of tiles.

Think of tiling your living room. The input T is a description of the various types of tile available, and the color-matching restriction reflects a rule enforced by your interior designer for esthetic reasons. The question we would like answered ahead of time is this: can *any* room, of any size, be tiled using only the available tile types, without violating the color-matching rule?

This algorithmic problem and its variants are commonly known as **tiling problems,** and are sometimes called **domino problems** because of the domino-like restriction on touching edges.

---

[1] After you finish reading this section you might want to try to convince yourself that this assumption is, in fact, necessary. We should add, however, that it is necessary only in the version we discuss here. It is easy to define a variant of the tiling problem, where instead of colors having to be identical, they have to match up in pairs (e.g. red against blue, green against orange, etc.). In such a version, the rotations-forbidden constraint is redundant, and the bad news is exactly the same.

In way of illustration, consider Fig. 2.2, which shows three tile types and a 5 × 5 tiling. The reader will have no difficulty verifying that the pattern in the figure can be extended in all directions, to yield a tiling of any sized room whatsoever. As can also be seen, this tiled portion uses only the three available types, and it adheres to the color-matching rule. However, exchange the bottom colors of tiles (2) and (3) as in Fig. 2.3, and the situation changes dramatically. It is now quite easy to show that even very small rooms cannot be tiled at all, since no matter how you attempt to lay down the tiles you will be forced very quickly into situations with mismatched colors. Figure 2.3 illustrates this. An algorithm for the tiling problem, thus should answer 'Yes' to the input consisting of the three tile types of Fig. 2.2, and 'No' to those of Fig. 2.3.

Can we somehow mechanize or 'algorithmicize' the reasoning employed in generating these answers?

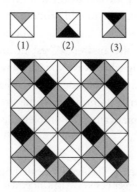

Fig. 2.2. Tile types that can tile any room, of any size.

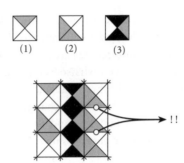

Fig. 2.3. Tile types that cannot tile even very small rooms.

The answer is no,[2] and this must be said in the strongest possible way:

> *There is no algorithm, and there never will be, for solving the tiling problem!*

You can try to devise one, and it might actually work quite well some of the time, on some of the inputs. Still, there will *always* be inputs upon which your algorithm will misbehave: it will either run forever and never halt, or will produce the wrong output.

This problem does not ask for a complicated output, such as a sample tiling when the answer is 'Yes', or an illustration of the impossibility of tiling when it is 'No'; all we want is a bare indication as to which of these is the case. Even so, the problem cannot be solved. And to repeat a point made in the Preamble, this fact has been proved mathematically. The problem has no solution and it never will. Period.

---

[2] H. Wang (1961). 'Proving Theorems by Pattern Recognition', *Bell Syst. Tech. J.* **40**, 1–42; R. Berger (1966). 'The Undecidability of the Domino Problem', *Memoirs Amer. Math. Soc.* **66**.

An algorithmic problem that admits no solution is termed **non-computable**; if it is a decision problem, as is the case here and in most of the examples that follow, it is termed **undecidable**. The tiling problem is thus undecidable: there is no way we can construct an algorithm, to be run on a computer, *any* computer, regardless of the amount of time and memory space required, that will be able to distinguish between tile types that can tile all areas and those that cannot.[3] This problem, then, lies above the line of Fig. 2.1.

do we really mean it?

Are we really claiming that this problem has no algorithmic solution at all? How can we justify drawing the grand line of Fig. 2.1? What gives us the right to use such all-inclusive terms like non-computable and undecidable? 'Maybe', the reader might claim, '*you* can't solve it, on your computer, with your ancient system software, mediocre programming language and old-fashioned algorithmic methods and tricks. But not me. I have an amazingly powerful supercomputer, I am smart and I work with incredibly sophisticated programming languages and state-of-the-art methodologies; *I* can surely do it! ... '.

---

[3] There is a subtly different version of the tiling problem. We asked whether the tile set T can be used to tile any finite area, of any size. Instead, we could have asked whether T can be used to tile the entire *infinite* two-dimensional plane. Interestingly, these two problems are completely equivalent: a 'Yes' for the first version is a 'Yes' for the second version too, and a 'No' for the first is a 'No' for the second too. One direction of this equivalence (if we can tile the entire infinite plane then we can tile any finite area) is trivial, but the argument that establishes the other direction is quite delicate. You are encouraged to try to find it. Thus, the infinite-plane version is also undecidable.

Well, no, dear reader, you cannot. When we label a problem non-computable or undecidable, we really and truly mean it. You can't solve it, and neither can anyone else, no matter how rich or patient or smart.

Still, the claim does sound very strange if we don't restrict the basic operations. Surely, if *anything* is allowed, the following two-step procedure solves the tiling problem:

1. If the tile types in the input set *T* can tile rooms of any size, output 'Yes' and stop;

2. Otherwise, output 'No' and stop.

So, is this not a solution? It consists of but two basic operations, and thus terminates in a finite amount of time, as it should. And surely it will always produce the correct output too.

Well, we must be a little more careful. Suppose we choose a fixed programming language *Lang* as the medium for expressing algorithms, and a fixed computer *Comp* as the machine on which they are to run (with the understanding that *Comp* can grant any amount of time, additional storage space, and any other tangible resource requested by a program during a computation). Suppose that we also agree that, for the moment, whenever we talk about an algorithm we really mean 'a program written in *Lang* and running on *Comp*'. With this setup, when we say 'no algorithm exists' we really mean that no program can be written in the specific language *Lang* for the specific computer *Comp*. This sounds a little less wild: it is conceivable that some problems will indeed be unsolvable if one is limited to working with a specific hardware/ software framework (sometimes called a **model of computation**). In fact, a reasonable way to dismiss the above two-line 'solution' to the tiling problem is to convince its proposers that there is no way to implement the test in line 1 using their chosen language *Lang* running on their machine *Comp*.

'OK', those proposing the two-line solution might say, 'so we can't solve the problem on this particular computer and with this particular language, but we *could* solve it had we a more powerful computer and a more sophisticated language.' Isn't the issue merely a question of coming up with the right algorithmic idea, designing the corresponding software and running it on a sufficiently powerful piece of hardware?[4]

No, it isn't. Not at all.

Actually, the situation is far more striking. It is not only that each model of computation can be shown to be fallible, by exhibiting some special problem it cannot solve, but there are *fixed* problems (the tiling problem is one of them) that are bad news for each and every model. That is, these problems are noncomputable regardless of the model chosen. They are thus *inherently* noncomputable. Worse, we computer scientists believe that this applies not only to currently known models, but to any effectively implementable language, running on any computer of any type, size or shape, *now or at any time in the future*. And this is what we mean when we say that a problem is noncomputable.

Amazingly, all that is needed in order to establish that a problem is noncomputable in this all-embracing sense is to show that it can't be solved within an extremely simple-looking model of computation, which we now set out to describe. That it actually can't be solved in *any* known model whatsoever, including the most

---

[4] This is probably what the *TIME* magazine interviewee quoted in the Preamble had in mind.

powerful computers invented and those that will be invented in the future, will follow from this modest-looking fact.

elementary computing devices

Let us see how simple we can make a general computing model.

The first thing to notice is that any item of data used by an algorithm can be viewed as a string of symbols. An integer is but a string of digits, and a fractional number is a string of digits with a decimal point. A word in English is a string of letters, and an entire text is really just a string of symbols consisting of letters, blanks, and punctuation marks. More complicated objects, such as lists, tables, city-connection networks, graphs, pictures, video sequences, and even whole databases, can also be encoded this way, by using special delimiting symbols to signify new items, line breaks, file borderlines, and so on.

The number of different symbols used in all such encodings is actually finite, and can always be fixed ahead of time. This is the ingenuity of a standard numbering scheme, such as the decimal system: we do not need infinitely many symbols, one for each number — 10 symbols suffice to encode them all.[5] The same obviously applies to words, texts, and pictures, since only a finite number of letters, punctuation marks, color codes, and special symbols are used in writing or in rendering images for computerization. Consequently, in principle, we can write any data of interest along a one-dimensional **tape**, perhaps a long one, which consists of a sequence of **squares**, each containing a single symbol taken from some finite **alphabet**. In order to allow for additional 'scrap paper'

---

[5] The binary system uses just two, 0 and 1.

to be used during the execution, the tape will be of unlimited length. We are not saying that it is *convenient* to work with data encoded in this primitive fashion, only that it is *possible* to do so.

So much for simplifying the data.

Now to the algorithmic/computational work itself. Instead of our device being able to do great things in manipulating data and computing thereon, we endow it with only the most trivial capabilities. It is allowed to look at one square of the tape at a time, examine the symbol it sees there, overwrite it with some other symbol of the finite alphabet if it wishes to, and move one square to the right or the left in preparation for its next action. To help the device decide which symbol to write and in what direction to move after the writing, it will be equipped with an extremely limited 'mind', in the form of a sort of gearbox, whose various positions — and there are only finitely many of them — are called **states**. At any given point in time, the device is said to be in one of the states (i.e. engaged in one of the gears), and depending on that state and the symbol it sees on the square it is looking at, it will make its decisions regarding how to rewrite the symbol it is looking at and whether to move to the left or the right.

The mechanism resulting from all this is called a **Turing machine**, after the British mathematician Alan M. Turing, who conceived of it in 1936.[6] A Turing machine is thus extremely simple (see Fig. 2.4). It chugs along a one-dimensional tape, one square at a time, in one of a finite number of gears, or states. In so doing, it uses an 'eye' of very limited power (actually called a **head**)

---

[6] A. Turing (1936). 'On Computable Numbers with an Application to the Entscheidungsproblem', *Proc. London Math. Soc.* **42**, 230–65. Corrections appeared in: *ibid.* (1937), **43**, 544–6.

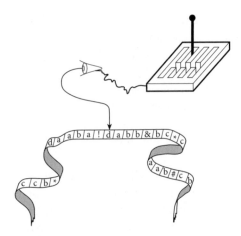

Fig. 2.4. A Turing machine.

to contemplate and possibly change the symbol it finds on the current square. It then 'changes gear', and hops over to a neighboring square for its next step. That's all.

Here is an informal description of a Turing machine that has been programmed to add two decimal numbers X and Y. (You can skip to the next section if you feel you might be bored by a rather tedious description of how a primitive-looking machine adds numbers.) The input numbers are given on the tape, separated by the symbol +, and the rest of the tape contains blanks, which are denoted here by #. See Fig. 2.5, which shows, from top to bottom, some snapshots of the tape as the computation proceeds.

Initially, the head is positioned at the leftmost symbol of the first number X — in this case, it is the 7. The machine then travels to the rightmost digit of X — the 6 — one square at a time, without making changes, until it reaches the separating symbol +, and then

Fig. 2.5. Adding numbers with a Turing machine.

moves one square to its left. It then erases this digit, i.e. replaces it
with a blank, while 'remembering' the erased digit as its state; it
will need 10 different states for this, one for each digit. The
machine then travels over to the rightmost digit of Y — the 9 —
and erases it too, entering a state that remembers the sum digit of
the two numbers, and whether or not there is a carry. This state
depends only on the current digit and the memorized one, and
hence 20 different states are needed — one for each of the possible
combinations of the 10 sum digits and the carry/no-carry indication. The machine then moves to the left of what remains of X and
writes the sum digit down — a 5 in this case — having prepared a
new separating symbol, say, an exclamation mark, '!'. This situation
is illustrated in the second line of the figure.

The next step is similar, but involves the *currently* rightmost digits (which were second from the right in the original numbers —
here the 3 and the 1), and takes the carry into account, if there is
one. The new sum digit — here 5 because of the carry — is written
down to the left of the previous one, and the process continues. Of
course, any one of the two input numbers might run out of digits
before the other, in which case, after adding the carry (if there is
one) to the remaining portion of the larger number, that portion is

just copied down on the left, tediously, digit by digit. Finally, a second exclamation mark is written down on the extreme left, to identify the machine's output as consisting of the portion of the tape enclosed by the two exclamation marks, and the machine halts.

Phew ...

the church-turing thesis

This example is a little surprising. Turing machines have only finitely many states, that is, a finite 'brain', and the only thing they can do is to rewrite symbols on a linear tape one at a time. Nevertheless, they can be programmed to add numbers of any size and shape. The task can be frustrating and thankless, and the machine's method of execution can be painfully slow and simple-minded (try to describe a Turing machine to *multiply* numbers or to compute the average of N salaries), yet it gets the job done.

With this in mind, let us forget about tedium, frustration and efficiency for the moment, and ask ourselves what indeed *can* be done with Turing machines, for whatever cost and no matter how painstakingly? Which algorithmic problems can be solved by an appropriately programmed Turing machine?

The answer to this is not a little surprising, but *very* surprising indeed: Turing machines are capable of solving any effectively solvable algorithmic problem! Put differently, any algorithmic problem for which we can find an algorithm that can be programmed in some programming language, *any* language, running on some computer, *any* computer — even one that has not been built yet (but, in principle, can be built), and even one that requires unbounded amounts of time and memory space for ever-larger inputs — is also solvable by a Turing machine!

This statement is one version of the so-called **Church–Turing thesis**, after Alonzo Church and Turing, who arrived at it independently in the 1930s, following the work of Kurt Gödel on the incompleteness of mathematics.[7]

It is important to realize that the CT thesis, as we shall call it (both for Church–Turing and for computability theory), is a thesis, not a theorem, since part of it cannot be proved mathematically. The reason for this is that one of the concepts it involves is informal and imprecise, namely, effective solvability, or **effective computability**. The thesis equates the mathematically precise notion of 'solvable by a Turing machine' with the informal, intuitive notion of 'effectively solvable', which alludes to all real computers and all programming languages, past, present, and future. It thus sounds more like a wild speculation than what it really is: a deep and far-reaching statement, put forward by two of the most respected pioneers of the science of computing. And, as we shall see, while its futuristic facet cannot be proved until the future materializes, its past and present facts *have* been proved.

Turing machines are a little like typewriters. A typewriter is also a very primitive kind of machine. All it enables us to do is to type sequences of symbols on blank paper. Yet despite this, any

---

[7] K. Gödel (1931). 'Über formal unentscheidbare Sätze der Principia Mathematica und verwandter Systeme, I', *Monatshefte für Mathematik und Physik* **38**, 173–98; A. Turing (1936). 'On Computable Numbers with an Application to the Entscheidungsproblem', *Proc. London Math. Soc.* **42**, 230–65; A. Church (1936). 'An Unsolvable Problem of Elementary Number Theory', *Amer. J. Math.* **58**, 345–63. See also S. C. Kleene (1981). 'Origins of Recursive Function Theory', *Ann. Hist. Comput.* **3**, 52–67, and M. Davis (1982). 'Why Gödel Didn't Have Church's Thesis', *Inf. and Cont.* **54**, 3–24.

typewriter can be used to type anything, even *Hamlet* or *War and Peace*. Of course, it might take a Shakespeare or a Tolstoy to 'instruct' the machine to do so, but it can be done. In analogy, it might take very talented people to program Turing machines to solve difficult algorithmic problems, but the basic model, so the CT thesis tells us, suffices for all problems that, in principle, *can* be solved by *some* device.

On the face of it, there is little reason to choose the Turing machine model to be the one the CT thesis mentions explicitly. The thesis might have talked about the model underlying a large IBM mainframe or a powerful Silicon Graphics workstation. In fact, one of the most striking formulations of the thesis doesn't mention a particular model at all, but states simply that all computers and all programming languages are equivalent in computational power, given unlimited computation time and memory space.

computability is robust

Why should we believe the CT thesis, when even its proponents admit that the yet-to-be-seen parts of it can't be proven? What evidence is there for it, and how does that evidence fare in an age of incredible day-to-day advances in both hardware and software?

Let us go back to the 1930s. At that time, several researchers were busy devising various algorithmic models, with the goal of trying to capture the slippery and elusive notion of effective computability, i.e. the ability to compute mechanically or electronically. Long before the first actual computers were invented, Turing suggested his limited-looking machines and Church devised a simple mathematical formalism of functions called the **lambda calculus**.

Around the same time, Emil Post defined certain symbol-manipulating mechanisms called **production systems**, and Stephen Kleene defined a class of mathematical objects called **recursive functions**. All these people tried, and succeeded, in showing that their models were able to solve many algorithmic problems for which 'effectively executable' algorithms were known. Actually, collectively, they also succeeded in showing that their formalisms were all equivalent in terms of the class of problems they could solve. Other people have since proposed numerous different models for the universal algorithmic device. Some of these models underly real computers, and some are purely mathematical in nature. But the crucial fact is that they have *all* been proven to be computationally equivalent; the class of algorithmic problems they can solve is the same. And this fact is still true today, even for the most powerful models conceived.[8]

Thus, the strongest, most powerful computer you know, coupled with the richest, most sophisticated programming language it supports, cannot do any more than can be done with a

---

[8] A. Turing (1936). 'On Computable Numbers with an Application to the Entscheidungsproblem', *Proc. London Math. Soc.* 42, 230–65; corrections appeared in: *ibid* (1937). 43, 544–6; A. Church (1936). 'An Unsolvable Problem of Elementary Number Theory', *Amer. J. Math.* 58, 345–63; S. C. Kleene (1935). 'A Theory of Positive Integers in Formal Logic', *Amer. J. Math.* 57, 153–73, 219–44; E. Post (1943). 'Formal Reductions of the General Combinatorial Decision Problem', *Amer. J. Math.* 65, 197–215; S. C. Kleene (1936). 'General Recursive Functions of Natural Numbers', *Math. Ann.* 112, 727–42. For proofs of the equivalence of these formalisms, see S. C. Kleene (1936). 'λ-Definability and Recursiveness', *Duke Math. J.* 2, 340–53; E. Post (1936). 'Finite Combinatory Processes — Formulation 1', *J. Symb. Logic* 1, 103–5; A. M. Turing (1937). 'Computability and λ-Definability', *J. Symb. Logic* 2, 153–63.

simple laptop and a very modest language. Or, for that matter, any more than can be done by the ultimate in computational simplicity — the ever so primitive Turing machine model.[9] Noncomputable (or undecidable) problems, such as the tiling problem, are solvable on neither, and computable (or decidable) problems, such as sorting words or testing a number for primality, are solvable on both. All this, mind you, on condition that running time and memory space are not an issue: there must be as much of those available as is needed.

This means that the class of computable, effectively solvable, or decidable algorithmic problems is, in fact, extremely *robust*. It is invariant under changes in the computer model, the operating system, the programming language, the software development methodology, etc. Proponents of a particular computer architec-

---

[9] Another extremely primitive model of computation that is nevertheless as powerful as Turing machines and is therefore also of universal power and subject to the CT thesis, is that of **counter programs**, or **counter machines**. A counter program is a sequence of simple instructions on non-negative integers that can assign 0 to a variable ($X \leftarrow 0$), and can increase or decrease a variable by one ($X \leftarrow Y + 1$ and $X \leftarrow Y - 1$). It can also branch conditionally, based on the zero-ness of a variable (**if** $X = 0$ **goto** G, where G labels some other instruction in the sequence). Surprisingly, merely incrementing and decrementing integers by 1 and testing values against 0 can be used to do anything any computer can do. Turing machines and counter programs are dual models in the following interesting sense: they both have access to unlimited amounts of memory, but in different ways. With Turing machines, the *number* of memory items (the tape's squares) is unlimited, but the *amount* of information in each is finite and is bounded ahead of time (one symbol from a fixed and finite alphabet). With counter programs it is the other way around: there are only finitely many variables in a given program, but each can contain an arbitrarily large number as its value, thus encoding a potentially unlimited amount of information.

ture or programming discipline must find reasons other than raw solving power to justify their recommendations, since anything doable with one is also doable with the other, and all are equivalent to the primitive machines of Turing or the various formalisms of Church, Post, Kleene, and others.

That so many people, working with such a diversity of tools and concepts, captured the very same notion (long before any actual computers were built, we should add!), is evidence for the profundity of that notion. That they were all after the same intuitive concept and ended up with different-looking, but equivalent, models, is justification for equating that intuitive notion with those precise models. Hence the CT thesis.

Thus, if we set efficiency aside for now, not caring about how *much* time or space an algorithm actually requires, but simply giving it anything it wants, the line drawn between the computable and the noncomputable in Fig. 2.1 is fully justified. Moreover, as we proceed in our discussions, we can safely allude to some favorite computer *Comp* and programming language *Lang* as the model on which algorithmic problems are to be solved, just as we did earlier on a temporary basis, because it makes no difference! Nevertheless, it is intellectually satisfying to be able to point to a most simple model — Turing machines — that is as powerful as anything of its kind.[10]

---

[10] Another advantage of knowing that simple-looking models like Turing machines or counter programs are universally powerful, is that they are better suited for establishing bad news. As stated earlier, to prove that a problem is undecidable, for example, all one has to show is that it cannot be solved using Turing machines. That it cannot be solved on *any* model will then follow from the CT thesis.

domino snakes

Let us return for a moment to the tiling problem. Some people react to its undecidability by saying: 'well, obviously the problem is undecidable, since a single input can give rise to a potentially infinite number of cases to check; and there is no way you can get an infinite job done by an algorithm that has to terminate after finitely many steps.' Indeed, a single input (that is, a single set T of tile types) apparently requires all rooms of all sizes to be checked (or, equivalently, a single infinite 'room'), and there appears to be no way to set a *bound* on the number of cases that have to be considered.

This unboundedness-implies-undecidability hypothesis is unbased, and can be very misleading. In fact, it is often simply wrong. To drive the point home, here is a similar tiling problem, whose status violates this hypothesis in a surprising way. As before, the input contains a finite set T of tile types, but here it also contains the coordinates of two points on the infinite plane, V and W. The problem doesn't talk about tiling whole rooms, but, in the spirit of real domino games, it asks if it is possible to connect V and W by a 'domino snake' consisting of tiles from T, and with the same color-matching restriction: every two adjacent edges must have identical colors (see Fig. 2.6). Note that a snake originating at V might twist and turn erratically, reaching unboundedly distant points before converging to W. So, to decide whether or not there is such a snake, we might have to check ever-larger portions of the infinite plane (the infinitely large room) — perhaps all of it — before we either find such a snake or conclude that none exists. Hence, this problem also seems to require an infinite search, prompting us to presume that it too is undecidable.

Fig. 2.6. A domino snake connecting *V* to *W*.

Curiously, the decidability of the domino snake problem depends on the portion of the plane available for placing tiles, and in a very counter-intuitive fashion. If snakes are allowed to go anywhere (that is, if the allowed portion is the entire infinite plane), the problem is decidable; but if the allowed area is limited to, say, the upper half of the plane, the problem becomes undecidable! That is, if snakes can run around anywhere, with *no* limitations, there *is* an algorithm to decide whether there is a snake going from *V* to *W*, but if we *do* limit its habitat, there is *no* algorithm. Surprising, right?

The latter case is 'more bounded' than the former, and therefore should be 'more decidable'. The facts, however, are quite the other way around.[11]

---

[11] If the available portion of the infinite plane is *finite*, the problem is trivially decidable, since only finitely many possible snakes can be positioned in a given finite area, and an algorithm can be easily designed
continued on next page

program verification

In Chapter 1 we discussed the need for algorithms and programs to be correct. Establishing the fact that a candidate program indeed solves the algorithmic problem you are working on is no easy feat. So it is tempting to ask whether computers can do this for us. We would really like an automatic *verifier*, a piece of software whose input consists of (the description of) an algorithmic problem and (the text of) an algorithm, or program. We would like the verifier to determine algorithmically whether the given program solves the given problem. In other words, we want a 'Yes' if for each of the input problem's legal inputs the input program, had we run it on that legal input, would terminate with the correct output, and a 'No' if for even a single legal input the input program would either fail to terminate or would terminate with the wrong output (see Fig. 2.7). The verifier must be able to do this

---

continued

to examine them all. Far more interesting is the fact that the snake domino problem has been proved to be undecidable for almost any conceivable *infinite* restriction of the plane, as long as the portion under consideration is unbounded in both directions. The most striking contrast is best described by saying that only a single point stands between decidability and undecidability, since the strongest result known is this: while the problem, as we have seen, is decidable in the whole plane, it becomes undecidable if even a *single point* is removed from the plane, meaning that candidate snakes are allowed to go anywhere except through a third given point, *U*. See H.-D. Ebbinghaus (1982). 'Undecidability of Some Domino Connectability Problems', *Zeitschr. Math. Logik und Grundlagen Math.* 28, 331–6; Y. Etzion-Petrushka, D. Harel, and D. Myers (1994). 'On the Solvability of Domino Snake Problems', *Theoret. Comput. Sci.* 131, 243–69.

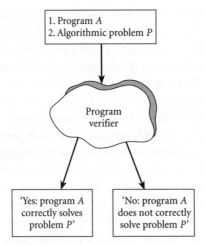

Fig. 2.7. A hypothetical program verifier.

for *every* choice of algorithmic problem and for every choice of a candidate program.[12]

As a particularly pressing example, wouldn't it be nice if someone were to establish a start-up company and construct a general-purpose Y2K verifier? We could have then subjected any piece of software to the verifier, and found out whether what it would have done on 1 January 2000 is the same as what it did on 31 December 1999. Is this possible?

---

[12] Here too, it is convenient to fix a computer model and programming language in advance. Actually, since in this case programs are part of the input, we *must* adopt a language with well-defined syntax and semantics, so as to be able to hand the program verifier a real, tangible object as input. By the CT thesis, however, such a choice does not detract from the generality of what we have to say here.

Well, the general verification problem is undecidable, as is the special case of verifying compliance with the year 2000. A candidate verifier might work nicely for many of its inputs; it might be able to verify certain kinds of programs against certain limited kinds of specifications, but as a general verifier it is bound to fail. There will always be algorithms or programs that such a verifier will not be able to verify. We can thus forget about a computerized solution to the Y2K problem or any other such sweeping attempt at establishing the correctness of software by computer.

In contrast to tiling and snake domino problems, which you might dismiss as toy problems of no practical value, program verification is an extremely important computer-related task, coming from the real world. The fact that it is unsolvable dashes our hope for a software system that would make sure that our computers do what we want them to.

the halting problem

It turns out that the news is as bad already for a lot less than the full correctness of programs. We cannot even decide whether a program merely terminates on its inputs. Worse, it is not even decidable whether it terminates on one specific input! These issues of termination, or halting, are at the heart of Problem 8 in the list given in Chapter 1, and they deserve special attention.

Consider the following algorithm (call it A):

1. while $X \neq 1$ do the following: set $X \leftarrow X - 2$;
2. stop.

In words, the algorithm A repeatedly decreases its input number X by 2 until it becomes equal to 1. Assuming that the legal inputs consist of the positive integers 1, 2, 3, etc., it is quite obvious that

A halts precisely for the *odd* numbers. An even number will be decreased repeatedly by 2, will 'miss' the 1, running forever through 0, –2, –4, –6, etc. Hence the problem of deciding whether a legal input will cause this particular algorithm to halt is trivial: all we have to do is to check whether the input is odd or even, and answer accordingly.

Here is a slightly more complicated algorithm, *B*:

1. while $X \neq 1$ do the following:

    1.1. if *X* is even, set $X \leftarrow X/2$;

    1.2. otherwise (i.e. *X* is odd), set $X \leftarrow 3X + 1$;

2. stop.

This algorithm repeatedly halves its input if it is even, but *increases* it more than threefold if it is odd. And it too halts if and when it reaches the value 1. For example, if *B* is run on the number 7, the sequence of values is: 7, 22, 11, 34, 17, 52, 26, 13, 40, 20, 10, 5, 16, 8, 4, 2, 1, as you can easily check, following which execution halts. Actually, if we try running algorithm *B* on an arbitrary positive integer, even using a powerful computer, we will find that it either terminates, or progresses through an erratic-looking sequence, reaching surprisingly high values, and fluctuating unpredictably. In the latter case, one gives up after a while, having not observed either termination or a periodic sequence of values (which, of course, would have indicated that the computation will not terminate). Indeed, over the years, *B* has been tested on numerous inputs, and on large and fast computers. On the one hand, no periodicity has been observed, and no-one has been able to come up with an input for which *B* can be *proved* not to terminate. On the other hand, no-one has been able to prove that *B* terminates for *all* positive integers (although people believe it does). Which of these is the case is actually a difficult unresolved question in the branch of mathematics known as **number theory**, and it has been open for some 60 years.[13]

So, here we are, with two algorithms, the uninteresting A and the far more interesting B. While some mathematicians in the field of number theory would probably give a lot to find out whether B halts on all its inputs, B is still but one specific algorithm. In the study of algorithmics we are not that interested in the halting behavior of specific programs, even tantalizing ones like B. Rather, we are interested in the generic problem of determining the halting behavior of an unknown given algorithm or program. This general decision problem is called the **halting problem**.

As input, the halting problem is fed the text of a legal program A in our chosen programming language *Lang*, and a potential input X, which is really nothing more than a string of symbols. The problem asks whether or not A would have terminated had we run it on the input X (see Figure 2.8).

The halting problem, just like the more demanding verification problem, cannot be solved by algorithmic means; it is undecidable. This means that there is no way to tell, in general, and in a finite amount of time, whether the execution of a given program will terminate on a given input.[14]

---

[13] J. C. Lagarias (1985). 'The $3x + 1$ Problem and its Generalizations', *Amer. Math. Monthly* **92**, 3–23. This is perhaps the simplest-to-describe open problem in mathematics. To understand it you need to know nothing except basic arithmetic symbols. Is it or is it not the case that *any* positive integer eventually reaches 1 if it is repeatedly halved when even and tripled and increased by one when odd?

[14] This is due to Turing. See his 1936 paper referenced in footnote 6 of this chapter. See also G. Rozenberg and A. Salomaa (1994). *Cornerstones of Undecidability*. Prentice Hall, New York, NY.

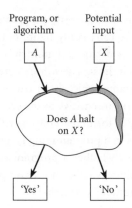

Program, or algorithm

Potential input

A

X

Does A halt on X?

'Yes'

'No'

Fig. 2.8. The halting problem.

It is tempting to try to solve the problem by a simulation algorithm that simply mimics running the program A on the input X and waits to see what happens. The point is that if and when execution terminates we can justifiably stop and conclude that the answer is 'Yes': had we indeed run A on X it would have terminated. The difficulty is in deciding when to stop waiting and say 'No'. We cannot simply give up after a long wait and conclude that since the simulation has not yet terminated it never will. Perhaps if we had left it to run just a little longer — maybe one more microsecond would do it — it *would* have terminated. Simulating the given program's behavior on the given input, therefore, does not do the job, and, as stated, nothing can do the job, since the problem is undecidable.

nothing about computation can be computed!

This phenomenon is actually much deeper and more devastating. There is a remarkable result, called **Rice's theorem**, that shows that not only can we not verify programs or determine their halting status, but we can't really figure out *anything* about them.[15] No algorithm can decide *any* nontrivial property of computations. More precisely, let us say we are interested in deciding some property of programs, which is (i) true of some programs but not of others, and (ii) insensitive to the syntax of the program, that is, it is a property of the underlying algorithm and not of the particular form it takes in a programming language. For example, we might want to know whether a program runs in less than a particular amount of time, whether it ever outputs a 'Yes', whether it always produces numbers, whether it is equivalent to some other program, etc., etc.

What Rice's theorem tells us is that *no* such properties of programs can be decided. They are *all* undecidable. We can really forget about being able to reason automatically about programs. Virtually *nothing* about computation is computable!

some problems are even worse

As it turns out, three of the undecidable problems mentioned so far — the tiling problem, the domino snake problem on the half-plane, and the halting problem – are **computationally equivalent**.[16] This is not a simple notion, since obviously these problems *look* very different: tiling rooms and determining whether pro-

---

[15] H. G. Rice (1953). 'Classes of recursively enumerable sets and their decision problems', *Trans. Amer. Math. Soc.* 74, 358–66.

[16] To be technically precise, the halting problem has to be negated for this equivalence to hold. In other words, the version that is equivalent to the others is the *non*-halting problem, in which we want a 'Yes' if the given program does *not* halt on the given input, and a 'No' if it does halt.

grams terminate, for example, don't seem to have anything to do with each other. In fact, they have *everything* to do with each other.

What exactly do we mean by two undecidable problems being computationally equivalent? Well, the key notion is inter-reducibility. Each one of the two problems is **reducible** to the other, in that sense that one can be decided with the aid of an imaginary solution, or **oracle**, for the other. Thus, if we had an algorithm to decide, in general, whether programs halt on inputs (we can't have a *real* algorithm for this because the problem is undecidable, but say we had a hypothetical one, the oracle) we could use it to decide whether tiles can tile living rooms. And perhaps more surprisingly, vice versa: if we could decide about tiling living rooms, we could decide about computer programs halting. Imagine that!

Having an imaginary solution is like having an immortal oracle who gives you answers to certain questions for free. Thus, if you had an oracle who could answer tiling questions whenever asked, you could solve the halting problem.

A rather striking addendum to the equivalence between these noncomputable problems is that some problems — program verification for example — are even *less* decidable. What on earth can we mean by this? What can be worse for an algorithmic problem than to have no solution at all? Here too, the key is reducibility: the halting problem can be reduced to program verification, meaning that an imaginary solution to the latter can be used to solve the former. The converse, however, is not true. Even with a free (imaginary) oracle for the halting problem, or the tiling problem, or the half-plane snake domino problem (or even with oracles for *all* of these) we could *not* verify programs. The verification problem is thus harder than the halting problem; it is less decidable, so to speak.

This oracle-based way of comparing undecidable problems, making some of them 'better' than others, induces a classification of algorithmic problems into levels of undecidability, or levels of noncomputability. Layers upon layers of problems exist, coming with worse and worse news! The three equivalent problems we mentioned, halting, tiling, and half-plane snakes, turn out to be on one of the lowest such levels. You might say that they are *almost* decidable. Sadly, however, many problems reside far higher up in the hierarchies of ever more terrible news, so that they are much less decidable than the ones lower down.

One interesting level is sometimes termed **high noncomputability**, or **high undecidability**, and it deserves a zone of its own in the sphere of algorithmic problems (see Fig. 2.9). Highly noncomputable problems are much, much worse than the 'ordinarily' noncomputable ones we have discussed. In fact, they are *infinitely* worse. Even an infinite lineup of increasingly more sophisticated oracles wouldn't suffice to solve them. Thus, above the almost

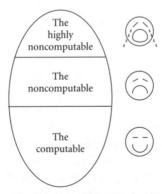

Fig. 2.9. The sphere of algorithmic problems: Version II.

computable, or almost decidable problems (tiling, halting, and their friends) there are infinitely many different problems, each more difficult than the ones lower down, and each one not computable even with the aid of oracles for all those below it. The problems we have termed highly undecidable are even worse than all those.[17]

* * *

---

[17] S. C. Kleene (1943). 'Recursive predicates and Quantifiers', *Trans. Amer. Math. Soc.* **53**, 41–73. The high undecidability we discuss here is called the Σ_1^1/Π_1^1 level, in technical terminology. A simple example of a highly undecidable problem is the following variant of the tiling problem (we use the version of tiling that asks whether the set T of tile types can tile the entire infinite plane, rather than the one that asks about tiling all finite areas). The new variant adds but a small requirement: we want to know whether T can tile the infinite plane, but in such a way that the tiling contains infinitely many copies of the first tile listed in T; i.e. a **recurrence** of the designated tile type. We want a 'Yes' if there is a T-tiling of the plane containing a recurrence of this particular tile, and a 'No' if no such tiling exists. Note that the answer must be 'No' even if there *are* legal tilings of the whole plane using the tiles in T, but none of them has the first tile of T recurring infinitely often. This extra requirement doesn't look as though it should make a big difference, because if you can tile the infinite plane using a finite set of tile types, then *some* of the types must occur in the tiling infinitely often. The difference is that here we want a *specific* tile to recur. Despite the apparent similarity, this **recurring dominoes** problem, as it is called, is highly undecidable. It is not decidable even with the use of imaginary solutions to the infinitely many other problems residing on lower levels of the undecidability hierarchies. See D. Harel (1986). 'Effective Transformations on Infinite Trees, with Applications to High Undecidability, Dominoes, and Fairness', *J Assoc. Comput. Mach.* **33**, 224–48. But don't think that this is as bad as it can get. Some problems are even worse than the highly undecidable ones, but we will ease off now, and let it go at that.

In summary, we have learned that the world of algorithmic/computational problems is divided into the computable, or decidable, vs. the noncomputable, or undecidable, and that among themselves the problems in the latter class exhibit various degrees of hardness. We have also seen that these facts are extremely robust and lasting: the dividing lines of Fig. 2.9 are mathematically precise and firmly defined, and are insensitive to variations in computational models, languages, methodologies, hardware or software.

So our hopes for computer omnipotence are shattered. We now know that not all algorithmic problems are solvable by computers, even with unlimited access to resources like time and memory space.

Can we finish our story here? Isn't this the bad news alluded to in the Preamble? What else can go wrong?

chapter 3

sometimes we can't afford to do it

The fact that some tasks cannot be computerized is bad enough already. But we are not done yet. Let us now concentrate on the ones that can.

Say we are asked to construct a bridge over a river. The bridge could be 'incorrect'; it might not be wide enough for the required lanes, it might not be strong enough to carry rush-hour traffic, or it might not reach the other side at all! However, even a 'correct' design may be unacceptable. It might call for too large a workforce, or too many materials or components. It might also require far too much time to bring to completion. In other words, although it will result in a good bridge, a design might be too *expensive*.

The field of algorithmics is susceptible to similar concerns. Even if a problem is computable, or decidable, and a correct solution algorithm is found, that algorithm might be far too costly in its use of resources, and hence impractical. The term 'impractical' sounds mild, but it's not: we shall discuss problems that require such formidable amounts of running time or memory space, as to become just as unsolvable as the ones of the previous chapter.

resources: time and memory space

Lumber, steel, screws, and bolts — the stuff of bridges – are not relevant here. Instead, we have the resources consumed by computer programs, particularly running time and memory space. These are often referred to as measures of **computational complexity**, and are called simply **time** and **space**. Time is measured by the number of basic actions carried out during an execution, and space by the area in the computer's memory required to store the data generated and manipulated in that execution. These depend on the computer running the algorithm, of course, an issue we shall return to later.

The amount of time and space used by an algorithm will typically differ from input to input, and algorithmic performance must be assessed accordingly. The salary summation algorithm clearly takes longer on lengthier lists, but this doesn't mean that its time performance cannot be formulated precisely; all it means is that the formulation will have to account for the fact that the running time depends on (is a function of), the length of the input list. The symbol N is often used generically to denote input size; if we say that an algorithm runs in time $5N$ we mean that it never performs more than 5 times N basic actions on any given input of size N.

The important thing is the input's *size*, not the input itself. The time it takes to multiply two integers should not be much different for pairs of inputs with the same number of digits, but will typically grow with longer numbers. The same goes for finding paths in city maps, for searching and sorting lists, etc.

Time is a crucial factor in computation. In many day-to-day applications there is vast room for improvement. Time is money, and computer time is no exception.[1] As to memory space, although in many cases this resource can be every bit (no pun intended) as crucial as time, we shall concentrate mostly on time complexity.

improving running time

Sometimes running time can be improved with simple tricks. Consider a straightforward procedure for seeking a name in a long list. We go through the names on the list one by one, repeatedly inspecting the current name to see if it is the one we are after, and then checking to see that we are not at the list's end before moving on to the next name. So we carry out two basic actions for each name we check. If the list is of length N, the time complexity is $2N$.

To improve things, we can start out by adding the sought-for name to the end of the list, in an artificial manner. If the name did not appear in the original list at all, it now appears once, at its end, and if it did it now appears twice, once in the original place and once at the end. What is the advantage of this addition? Well, it enables us to expedite the entire process, by omitting the end-of-list check that was carried out again and again, for each name inspected. Now that the sought-for name appears at the end, we are bound to bump into it even if it were not in the original list.

---

[1] In fact, where computers are concerned, time can be absolutely critical: certain kinds of computerized applications involve **real-time systems**, especially those found in the aerospace and defense industry, and even in automobiles. They must respond to external stimuli in 'real time', since failing to do so could be fatal.

Once we find it, we check just once if we are at the list's end. If we are, we may safely conclude that the name did not originally appear; and if we are not at the list's end, then the place we are at right now is the original appearance of the name in the list.

This yields a 50% improvement in time: assuming that the inspection of a name costs roughly the same as checking whether we are at the end of the list — one basic action — the running time drops from $2N$ to around N. Both versions work their way through the list item by item. In both cases, if the sought-for name is not on the list, or if it happens to be positioned last, we will have to inspect all the N names. The difference is in how much each inspection costs.

An important point is that the $2N$ for the first version and the N for the second are both **worst case** estimates. That is, there are 'bad' inputs (the ones where the name does not appear in the list at all) that force the algorithm to indeed run through the entire list. In other words, the algorithm could presumably run for much less on certain inputs (those in which the name appears early in the list), perhaps on *most* inputs, but it never runs for more, even on the worst input of its size. We shall stick to worst case complexity throughout most of the book.[2]

Now, although the two algorithms for the name-searching problem differ by a factor of 2, both run in time that is *propor-*

---

[2] Worst case analysis is not the only way to view time complexity. People also study and analyze algorithms for their **average case** time performance, obtaining insight into the duration of an algorithm's run on a *typical* input. This analysis can cause unpleasant surprises, however, since running the algorithm on a bad input can take much longer than the average case predicts. In any case, as mentioned, we shall concentrate on the worst case.

tional to *N*. The running time grows *linearly* with *N*. When the worst case running time of an algorithm is proportional to the length of the input, we say that it runs in **linear time**. This phrase blurs the distinction between *N* and 2*N*, so that with this terminology it is as if the 50% trick doesn't make a real difference; we have a linear-time algorithm either way.[3]

Impressive as a 50% cut in running time sounds, we can often do much better. When we say better, we don't mean just fixed-rate improvements of 50%, 60%, or even 90%, which would all retain the linear-time status of an algorithm, but ones whose *rate* gets increasingly better as the size of the input increases. These are **order of magnitude** improvements.

One of the best-known examples of this involves searching for a name, as before, but this time in an ordered, or *sorted* list; say, a telephone book with the names ordered lexicographically. Here, the naïve linear search can be dramatically improved. Instead of simply going through the names in some order, one by one, the idea is to use a splitting technique, whereby the first name we inspect is the one appearing smack in the middle of the list. If this does not turn out to be the name we are after, then, depending on whether it is lexicographically larger or smaller than the sought-for name, we can discard the entire first or second half of the list, concentrating our search on the remaining half only. In this way we manage to decrease the size of the problem to half of its original size, by inspecting a single name only. We now do the same to the remaining half: we inspect *its* middle name and compare it to

---

[3] The term 'linear time' applies to any algorithm whose running time is bounded from above by *KN* for some constant *K* > 0. Thus, even *N*/100 is linear time. There is a special notation for this: *O(N)*, read 'big-O of *N*', or 'order of *N*'.

the sought-for name, thus reducing the size of the problem to a *quarter* of the original size. Half of this half-list is discarded and the middle name of the remaining portion is inspected; and so on. When the ever-decreasing portion in hand gets so small as to contain only one name and this too is not the one we are looking for, the search ends in failure. This **binary search** algorithm works by a divide and conquer kind of principle: you repeatedly halve the list, check the middle name, and are then left with having to 'conquer' only one of the resulting half-lists.

Binary search runs in time proportional to $\log_2 N$, the base-2 logarithm of N, in the worst case. We thus say that it is a **logarithmic-time** algorithm.[4] The precise mathematical definition of the logarithmic function is not important here, so don't feel bad if you are not familiar with it, but what *is* important is that logarithmic time embodies an incredible improvement over linear time. One that is not only better by some constant factor of 50% or 90%, but is better in the order of magnitude sense of the word. The improvement *itself* grows rapidly with the growth of N, as the following table shows:

Length of List, N	Number of comparison, $\log_2 N$
10	4
100	7
1000	10
1 000 000	20
1000 000 000	30
10^{18}	60

[4] The words 'logarithm' and 'algorithm' are not related.

Consider this: to find a number in New York City's telephone book, which must have around a million names, you don't need to inspect more than 20 numbers! For a telephone book with a billion names (China's, perhaps, or maybe the whole world's?), you need inspect only 30. Even with the overhead required to halve the lists and keep track of where we are searching, this is a very, *very* fast algorithm.

upper and lower bounds

The **sorting problem**, Problem 4 on the list of Chapter 1, is another case where the time complexity of a naïve algorithm can be vastly improved. We can think of it as asking for a method of transforming a jumbled telephone book into an ordered one.

An obvious sorting method that comes to mind is to repeatedly find the smallest element in the list, output it, and remove it from the list, in preparation for a search for the next smallest one. In the worst case, this process takes about $N^2/2$ comparisons, which is proportional to N-squared (that is, to N^2), and is thus termed **quadratic time**. However, there are several more sophisticated algorithms for sorting, with such names as **heapsort** and **mergesort**.[5] These are much faster. They run in time proportional to N times the logarithm of N, or in symbols $N \log_2 N$, rather than N^2, which is a vast improvement: using these methods, a jumbled New York City telephone book can be arranged in lexicographical

---

[5] See D. E. Knuth (1973). *The Art of Computer Programming*, Vol. 3: *Sorting and Searching*. Addison-Wesley, Reading, MA, 2nd ed. 1998; T. H. Cormen, C. E. Leiserson, and R. L. Rivest (1990). *Introduction to Algorithms*. MIT Press, Cambridge, MA.

order using only several million comparisons, instead of many billions.[6]

So we can search for a name in an ordered list in logarithmic time, and we can sort an unsorted list in less than quadratic time. Fine. But can we do better? Is it possible to search for an element in a million-name telephone book with *less* than 20 comparisons in the worst case? Is there some unknown search algorithm out there that requires time of only, say, the square root of the logarithm of N in the worst case? How about sorting? Can we sort a list in, say, linear time, rather than in time $N \log_2 N$?

To put these questions into perspective, think of an algorithmic problem as sitting out there, possessing an inherent optimal solution, which is what we are after. Along comes someone with, say, a quadratic-time algorithm. Once we become convinced that the algorithm is correct, i.e. it indeed solves the problem, we know for sure that the optimal solution can't be any *worse* than quadratic

---

[6] Time complexity is obviously a relative concept that makes sense only in conjunction with an agreed-upon set of basic instructions. In the case of searching and sorting these typically include comparisons of names and numbers. Coding an algorithm in a specific language, or using a specific compiler, can obviously make a difference in the final running time. But on the assumption that algorithms are designed to use conventional basic instructions, the differences will most often be in the constant factor that is hidden in the term 'order-of-magnitude' (the big-O notation mentioned in an earlier footnote), so that the order-of-magnitude time complexity will not be affected. This robustness, coupled with the fact that, in the majority of cases, algorithms that are better in the order-of-magnitude sense are also better in practice, renders the study of order-of-magnitude time complexity the most interesting to computer scientists. Keep in mind, however, that this approach may hide issues of possible practical importance, such as constant factors.

time. We have a quadratic time solution. We then say that we have approached the desired inherent optimum *from above*. Later on, someone else discovers a better algorithm, running, say, in time $N \log_2 N$, thus coming closer to the desired optimum, also from above. We now know that the problem cannot be inherently worse than that; the previous algorithm becomes obsolete, and the process continues. Accordingly, an efficient algorithm is said to place an **upper bound** on the algorithmic problem. Better algorithms approach the problem's best-known time bound from above, pushing it downward, closer to the unknown inherent complexity of the problem itself.

But how far can these improvements go? Can we approach the optimal complexity from *below*? What we are after is a **lower bound**, which would mean finding, not an algorithm, but a *proof* that you can't do any better. If we can prove rigorously that our problem cannot be solved by any algorithm that uses *less* than, say, logarithmic time (in the worst case), we can stop trying to find better algorithms, for there aren't any. Such a proof constitutes a lower bound on the algorithmic problem, in that *no* algorithm can bring about an improvement, and it doesn't matter how clever we are or how hard we work on devising one.

Discovering a fast algorithm shows that the problem's inherent time performance is no *worse* than some bound, while discovering a lower bound proof shows that it is no *better* than some bound. In both cases, a property of the algorithmic problem has been discovered, not a property of a particular algorithm. This is a subtle and confusing difference that is worth carefully taking in. Establishing a lower bound on a problem entails somehow considering *all* possible algorithms for it, while an upper bound is achieved by constructing one particular algorithm.

Lower bound proofs can be difficult to come by, but once found they put an end to futile attempts to search for better algorithms. Such bounds have been established for searching and sorting, for example. Searching in an ordered list has a lower bound of logarithmic time, so that the binary search algorithm is optimal. There simply *is* no better algorithm, and that's that. Similarly, sorting has a lower bound of $N \log_2 N$, so algorithms that achieve this running time, such as heapsort and mergesort, are optimal too. We thus say that searching and sorting are **closed problems**.[7] We have discovered their inherent time-complexity. End of quest.

Many algorithmic problems are not yet closed. Their upper and lower bounds do not meet, and we say that they give rise to **algorithmic gaps**. In the next chapter we shall see striking examples of gaps that are unacceptably large. For now, however, it suffices to realize that if a problem is not closed, the deficiency is not in the problem, but in our knowledge about it. We have failed either in finding the best algorithm for it or in proving that a better one

---

[7] The terms 'optimal solution' and 'closed problem' are used here in the order-of-magnitude sense. Matching upper and lower bounds means that we have found the optimum to within a constant factor. This still leaves open the possibility of improvements of the 50% and 90% kind, or improvements in other resources, such as space. Moreover, the lower bounds for searching and sorting are based on models of computation in which information about the input can be obtained only by comparing elements. If we know more about the input, the lower bound argument might fail, and a better algorithm may be found. As an extreme example, if we are told that the inputs to the sorting problem will always be distinct integers between 1 and some number M, linearly related to the length of the input list, we can sort in linear time: simply prepare an indexed array of length M, put each incoming number directly in its corresponding place and then read off the nonempty values in the resulting array as output.

does not exist, or in both. The inherent 'truth' is indeed out there somewhere; it is either the upper bound or the lower bound, or resides somewhere in between.

so what?

So we know that algorithmic problems will often admit solutions that are more time-efficient than the naïve approaches. A sorted list can be searched in logarithmic time, and we can sort a list in far less than quadratic time. In general, there are often more efficient algorithms to be found. So what?

Computers are the ones who have to carry out algorithms, you might think, and computers are fast. You might claim to be sufficiently 'rich' to afford to pay a million or a billion comparisons for searching through a list, and that a few extra seconds of computer time make no difference. If worst comes to worst, you could be saying to yourself, there are always faster machines to be bought. With this attitude, algorithmic gaps might not be bothersome either. So we don't know the exact optimal solution to our problem; so what? Once a reasonably good algorithm has been found, we may not be interested in better algorithms or in proofs that they don't exist.

Is the whole issue of algorithmic efficiency a tempest in a teacup?

the towers of Hanoi

Let us start answering this question by way of a rather playful puzzle example: it is known as the Towers of Hanoi.

We are given three towers, or pegs, *A*, *B*, and *C*. Three rings are piled in descending size on the first peg, *A*, and the other pegs are empty (see Fig. 3.1). We want to move the rings from *A* to one of the other pegs, perhaps using the third peg in the process. The rule is that rings are to be moved one at a time, but a larger ring may never be placed atop a smaller one.

This puzzle can be solved in seven steps, as follows:

> move the top ring from *A* to *B*;
> move the top ring from *A* to *C*;
> move the top ring from *B* to *C*;
> move the top ring from *A* to *B*;
> move the top ring from *C* to *A*;
> move the top ring from *C* to *B*;
> move the top ring from *A* to *B*.

It is not difficult to see that this series of actions really does the job; it complies with the rules of the game, and results in the rings all piled on peg *B*. Try to solve the same puzzle with four rings on peg *A*, not three (the number of pegs does not change). It shouldn't take you too long to find a sequence of 15-move instructions for this case.

Such puzzles may be entertaining and challenging, but our business is algorithmics, not puzzles. We are far more interested in the

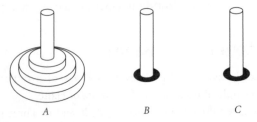

Fig. 3.1. The Towers of Hanoi.

general problem associated with the Towers of Hanoi than with this or that particular instance. The input to this algorithmic problem is any positive integer N, and a solution algorithm is required to issue a list of move instructions that will solve the puzzle for N rings. Once we have such an algorithm, any individual Towers of Hanoi puzzle, be it the 3-ring, the 4-ring, or 3178-ring version, can be solved by simply running the algorithm with the appropriate number of rings as input.

As it happens, there is a very simple algorithm for this, which can be carried out even by a small child.[8] To describe it, assume that the three pegs are arranged in a circle (the names of the pegs are unimportant):

1. do the following repeatedly, until step 1.2 can no longer be carried out:

    1.1. move the smallest ring to the peg residing next to it in clockwise order;

    1.2. make the only legal move possible that does not involve the smallest ring;

2. stop.

Step 1.2 means moving some ring other than the very smallest one to some peg other than the one it is on right now. Of course, this must be done in such a way that the ring moved is laid on top of a larger ring. The only situation in which this step *cannot* be carried out is when all the rings have been correctly transferred to some other peg; no ring is then exposed except the smallest. Note that when step 1.2 *can* be carried out, it is well defined and unambigu-

---

[8] P. Buneman and L. Levy (1980). 'The Towers of Hanoi Problem', *Inf. Proc. Lett.* **10**, 243–4.

ous, since *one* of the pegs has to have the smallest ring on top, and of the two remaining pegs one has a smaller ring on top than the other (or the other one has no rings on it at all). Thus, the only move not involving the smallest ring is to transfer that smaller ring to the other peg.

A time analysis of this algorithm shows that the number of single-ring moves it produces is precisely $2^N - 1$, that is, 1 less than 2 to the power of N (2 times itself N times). Since N appears in the exponent, such a function is termed **exponential**. It can be shown that $2^N - 1$ is also a *lower* bound for this problem: there is no way to get N rings transferred adhering to the rules, with less than $2^N - 1$ move instructions. Hence, our solution is optimal.

But is it a *good* solution? Being optimal in our business doesn't necessarily mean you are happy, only that you can't do any better. Is $2^N - 1$ a good time bound, like N or $N \log_2 N$? Maybe it is even a truly excellent one like $\log_2 N$.

By way of answering these questions, we should mention that the original version of the puzzle had the same three pegs, and it involved not three rings, but 64, moved by Tibetan monks. Given the $2^N - 1$ time complexity, even if the monks were to brush up their act and move a million rings every second, it would still take them more than half a million years to complete the 64-ring process! If, somewhat more realistically, they were to move one ring every five seconds, it would take them almost three trillion years to get the job done. No wonder they believed the world would end before they managed to finish. The Towers of Hanoi problem, at least for 64 rings or more, is thus hopelessly time-consuming.

Bad news indeed.

Somehow, this statement leaves us feeling somewhat unconvinced. It doesn't seem to signify real bad news in the world of computing as much as it illustrates the fact that the *output* here happens to be very long. For better or for worse, the puzzle has been set up in a way that requires $2^N - 1$ actions to get N rings transferred, and the algorithmic problem asks for a list of these actions. The computations themselves are extremely easy; it is the *output* that is long. To exhibit such a seemingly boring pheno-menon, we could have discussed a 'problem' that inputs N and asks for a printout of $2^N - 1$ copies of the letter a. That too would take time $2^N - 1$, and couldn't be done in less.

So our question is really this: does such devastating time per-formance, requiring zillions of years of running time, show up only when the outputs are devastatingly lengthy? Can we find problems with *short* outputs that behave as badly? How about decision problems? An algorithm that says only 'Yes' or 'No' spends all of its time *reaching* a verdict, not issuing it. Can such problems be that bad too?

Before we go any further, we should take a closer look at the kind of truly formidable time behavior represented by the likes of $2^N - 1$.

the good, the bad, and the ugly

Exponential functions, such as 2^N, yield very large numbers much sooner than linear or quadratic ones. Say N is 100. Then N^2 will be only 10 000, whereas 2^N is an *enormous* number; it is far, far larger than the number of microseconds that have elapsed since the Big Bang (see Fig. 3.2). In fact, exponential functions easily dwarf all **polynomial** functions, which are those of the form N^K for some fixed number K, like N^2 or N^{15}. It is true that N^{100}, for example, is larger than 2^N for all the values of N up to some point (996, to be

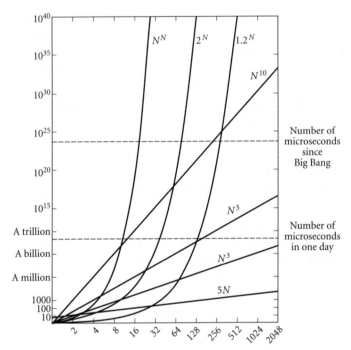

Fig. 3.2. Polynomial vs. exponential growth.

precise). However, from that point on, 2^N starts leaving N^{100} far behind, very, very quickly. And this is true for any choice of a fixed K.

Other functions exhibit similarly unacceptable growth rates. For example, $N!$, which is called N-**factorial**, and is defined as $1 \times 2 \times 3 \times \ldots \times N$, grows much faster than even 2^N. And the function N^N, which is N times itself N times, grows even faster than that. If N is 20, the value of 2^N is over a million (1 048 576, to be precise[9]), the value of $N!$ is well over 2 billion billions, and the value of N^N is more than 104 trillion trillions. If N is 150, the value of 2^N is billions of times larger than the number of protons in the entire known universe, and $N!$ and N^N cause that number to be reached for much smaller values of N.

Figure 3.2 shows the relative growth rates of some of these. It is a special kind of graph (termed logarithmic), in which the axes grow exponentially instead of linearly. This has the effect of causing all polynomials to come out as straight lines but exponentials to curve wildly upwards. Admittedly, this is something of a visual enhancement, but it serves nicely to show the difference between the two families of functions under discussion.[10]

Let us see what happens when such functions represent the time complexity of algorithms. The following table shows the running times of four algorithms on various quite modest input sizes. It assumes that they are run on a computer capable of a million instructions per second:

---

[9] This is closely related to the fact, mentioned earlier in searching New York's telephone book, that the logarithm of a million (with the fractional part dropped) is 20, since 2^N relates to N exactly as N does to $\log_2 N$.

[10] H. R. Lewis and C. H. Papadimitriou (1978). 'The Efficiency of Algorithms', *Scientific American* 238(1), 96–109; L. J. Stockmeyer and A. K. Chandra (1979). 'Intrinsically Difficult Problems', *Scientific American* 240(5), 124–33.

		Input length			
	10	**20**	**50**	**100**	**200**
N^2	1/10 000 second	1/2500 second	1/400 second	1/100 second	1/25 second
N^5	1/10 second	3.2 seconds	5.2 minutes	2.8 hours	3.7 days
2^N	1/1000 second	1 second	35.7 years	Over 400 trillion centuries	A 45-digit no. of centuries
N^N	2.8 hours	3.3 trillion years	A 70-digit no. of centuries	A 185-digit no. of centuries	A 445-digit no. of centuries

For comparison, the Big Bang was 12–15 billion years ago.

The first two lines in the table represent two typical polynomials, N^2 and N^5. The last two are exponential. Our point is that these two pairs are acutely different. The running time behaviors of the former are reasonable and we can live with them. The latter two are not and we can't.

Admittedly, the N^5 algorithm indeed behaves quite badly on an input of size 200, but with a faster machine and some tight optimization techniques we would probably be able to decrease the 3.7 days by a factor of 10 or so, and the task would become manageable. But now take a look at the *bad* algorithms, the 2^N and N^N ones. Even the faster of the two is so incredibly time-consuming as to require, in the worse case, 400 trillion centuries for a single input of size 100. For larger inputs (even only moderately larger), it is far, far slower than that. Worse functions, like N^N, give rise to this kind of devastating news much earlier, i.e. for much smaller inputs.

The really nasty parts of this table cannot be overcome by clever tricks, neat programming languages, or snazzy Web page designs on the Internet. Even a fully interactive, user-friendly, graphical, object-oriented, distributed approach (to use some fashionable buzzwords), full of bells and whistles, will have no noticeable effect.

Faster hardware doesn't help either. You might not like our assumption of one instruction per microsecond, claiming that, even as we speak, faster computers are available and more are in the making. Well, even if we had a machine 10 000 times faster (and this is not something that will happen overnight), the changes in the interesting parts of the table would be laughably marginal. For example, the entry labeled 'a 185-digit number of centuries' for an N^N-time algorithm running on an input of size 100, would have to be replaced by 'a 180-digit number of centuries'. Big deal, as the phrase goes. More significantly, it would take only a very slight increase in the size of the input to make the 10 000-fold faster computer run for the *same* 185-digit number of centuries: we need only go from size 100 to size 102. That's all. And this is exactly what the steepness of the curves in Fig. 3.2 is all about.

All this leads to a fundamental classification of time complexity functions, into 'good' and 'bad'. The good ones are the polynomial functions (more precisely, the ones bounded from above by a polynomial) and the bad ones are all the rest, sometimes termed **super-polynomial**.[11] Thus, logarithmic, linear and quadratic functions,

---

[11] We abuse conventional terminology slightly by using the term super-polynomial when we should really say exponential. That this is an abuse stems from the fact that there are functions, like $N^{\log_2 N}$ for example, that are super-polynomial but not quite exponential. The following papers first recognized the importance of the dichotomy between polynomial and super-polynomial time: M. O. Rabin (1960). 'Degree of Difficulty of Computing a Function and a Partial Ordering of Recursive Sets',

continued on next page

for example, are good, as is $N \log_2 N$, whereas ones like 2^N, $N!$, and N^N are bad. Later we shall see functions that are even worse, and those will be really, *really* ugly.

intractability

An algorithm or program whose worst-case time performance is captured by a good (i.e. polynomial) function in the size of its inputs is called a **polynomial-time algorithm**. An algorithm that, in the worst case, requires super-polynomial time, is thus bad. This is the classification for an algorithm.

We also want to classify algorithmic *problems* in terms of whether or not they can be solved by good algorithms, and here we must take into account all possible solutions. Accordingly, an algorithmic problem that admits a good algorithm as a solution is said to be **tractable,** whereas a problem that is solvable but admits only bad solutions is termed **intractable.** It is worth re-emphasizing that to label an algorithmic problem intractable we must have a proof that there is no good algorithm for it — not only among those we have discovered. There are none at all. Not even awaiting discovery. Simply failing to discover a polynomial-time algorithm for a problem can render it a *candidate* for intractability, but for it

---

continued
Technical Report No. 2, Hebrew University, Branch of Applied Logic, Jerusalem; A. Cobham (1965). 'The Intrinsic Computational Difficulty of Functions', *Proc. 1964 Int. Congress for Logic, Methodology, and Phil. of Sci.* (Y. Bar-Hillel, ed.). North Holland, 24–30; J. Edmonds (1965). 'Paths, Trees, and Flowers', *Canad. J. Math.* 17, 449–67; J. Hartmanis and R. E. Stearns (1965). 'On the Computational Complexity of Algorithms', *Trans. Amer. Math. Soc.* 117, 285–306.

to actually become intractable requires a *proved* lower bound of exponential-time.

The numbers and charts in the previous section are intended to support this dichotomy. Intractable problems require hopelessly large amounts of time even on relatively small inputs, which is not the case for tractable problems.

Actually, this is not quite as clear-cut as all that, and one can question the wisdom of drawing the line precisely where we did. We have already mentioned that an algorithm with time complexity N^{100} (which is good by our definition) is worse than an algorithm with the bad complexity 2^N for inputs of size 996 or less, and the turning point is much larger if we compare N^{100} with, say, 1.001^N, which is still termed bad. Nevertheless, the majority of bad algorithms are really not very useful, and most good ones are sufficiently useful to warrant the distinction made. The truth is that the majority of polynomial-time algorithms for real applications usually have quadratic time or cubic time complexity, i.e. N^2 or N^3, and not N^{100}. Similarly, you won't find intractable problems whose best algorithms are of complexity 1.001^N. Rather, they have complexities like 2^N or $N!$, or worse.

There is another thing, though. Recall the Church–Turing thesis, which asserts that the class of computable problems is robust, being insensitive to the differences between models of computation. This justified the line drawn in Fig. 2.1. The truth is that, in general, models of computation are **polynomially related**, meaning that not only can a problem that is solvable in your model be solved in mine too, but the difference in running time will be polynomial, i.e. good. My machine might be far slower than yours. It could be 10 times or 100 times slower, or it could take time that is the square of yours, or yours raised to the third or fifth power. But it doesn't take *exponentially* more time. What's good on yours is good on mine too.

This applies even to primitive models such as Turing machines. Despite being discouragingly slow, having to shuttle back and forth along a tape, remembering and changing single symbols, Turing machines are not *unreasonably* slow. They are only polynomially less efficient than even the fastest and most intricate computers, working with the most advanced languages, techniques and software.

The conclusion is this: not only is the class of *computable* problems robust, but so is the class of *tractable* problems. This is a refinement of the CT thesis that takes running time into consideration too, and is sometimes called the **sequential computation thesis**.

What is good is good everywhere, and what is bad is bad everywhere, or, paraphrasing the famous nursery rhyme about the brave old Duke of York:[12]

> *And when they are up they are up*
> *And when they are down they are down*

Now a reservation. Unlike the CT thesis, for which there isn't a shred of evidence that we might have to revise our beliefs at some point in the future, here there is a shade of doubt. The relatively new and exciting area of **quantum computing** seems poised to offer a possible challenge to the sequential computation thesis. There is a chance (a very small one, if you count the researchers

---

[12] See W. S. Baring-Gould and C. Baring-Goul (1962). *Annotated Mother Goose*, Clarkson N. Potter, New York, p. 138. (Many people misquote, calling him the *grand* old Duke of York.)

who think so), that this model of computation will manage to turn intractable problems into ones that are tractable and manageable in practice. We shall discuss this further in Chapter 5. However, even if this happens, it is still a very long way off, so for now we shall proceed with this stronger thesis intact, and with the knowledge that tractability is a strong and robust notion, insensitive to anything we know about now.

The sphere of algorithmic problems that appeared in Fig. 2.1 now gets what we might term a 'facedrop', and a third dividing line is added; see Fig. 3.3. The new line is the most important one, since it separates problems that can be solved in practice from those that cannot. It doesn't make much difference if your problem is undecidable or 'merely' intractable — either way you won't be able to solve it, at least in the puristic worst-case sense of 'has to work correctly and efficiently for each and every possible input'.

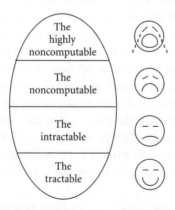

Fig. 3.3. The sphere of algorithmic problems: Version III.

roadblocks and chess

All this sounds very nice in theory. We have solvable and unsolvable problems, and within the former we have a subdivision that labels as bad those that do not give rise to polynomial-time solutions. But maybe there aren't any such cases unless the outputs are required to be unreasonably long. Do inherently intractable problems even exist, or are all decidable and computable problems also tractable? Are there problems with *proven* lower bounds of exponential time, whose intractability is not the result of their need to pour forth exponentially long outputs, but, rather, is inherent in their very computational nature?

The answer is a resounding yes. Just as there are many problems that are undecidable, so are there many problems that have been proved to require wholly unreasonable time to solve, using any algorithm, running on any kind of machine.

Here is an example; again, a rather playful one like tiling rooms. It is called Roadblock. It is played by two players, Alice and Bob, on a network of intersecting roads, each road segment colored with one of several colors. Certain intersections are marked '*Alice wins*' or '*Bob wins*', and each player owns a fleet of cars occupying certain intersections. In his or her turn, a player may move one self-owned car along a stretch of road to a new intersection. There are two restrictions: (i) all intersections along the stretch must be free of cars, including the player's own cars and including the target intersection, and (ii) the player has to stick to one color in each turn, and can switch colors of the road segments only in the next turn. The winner is the first player to reach one of his or her winning points.

The input to the Roadblock problem is a description of a network, with cars placed at certain intersections. The problem asks whether Alice (whose turn it is) has a winning strategy.[13] Figure 3.4 shows a Roadblock configuration in which the circled 'A's and 'B's mark the locations of Alice's and Bob's cars, respectively, and different line types denote different colors. For this particular input, that is, starting from this particular configuration with Alice to move, she can win no matter what Bob does (how?). Notice that this is a decision problem; we are not asking how, just whether. All we want is a 'Yes' or a 'No'.

The Roadblock problem has been proved to have a 2^N lower bound on time. The size N of the input is the number of intersections in the network. Thus, while smallish Roadblock configurations might be easy to analyze (e.g. that of Fig. 3.4), and some

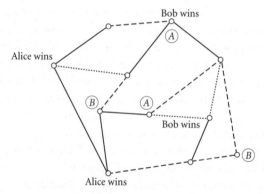

Fig. 3.4. A Roadblock configuration that Alice can win.

---

[13] A winning strategy in a game is a recipe (actually an algorithm) for the starting player, which prescribes a move for him or her to make for every one of his or her opponent's moves, such that no matter what the opponent chooses to do at each stage the starting player is guaranteed to win eventually.

larger ones might not be too difficult either, the worse-case performance of *any* algorithm whatsoever will be absolutely terrible: for the very best algorithm we might design, there will always be reasonably sized configurations that will cause it to run for an unacceptable amount of time.[14]

Thus, there is no practical algorithmic method, and there never will be, for determining in general whether a given player has a guaranteed strategy for winning a Roadblock game. And notice that this is the decision problem version: if we wanted to *see* Alice's winning strategy if she has one, or an example of Bob's possible win if she doesn't, things would be at least as bad as this, possibly even worse.

Since we are talking about games and winning strategies, consider the corresponding problem for chess. Does white have a guaranteed winning strategy from a given chess configuration? Interestingly, although chess is clearly a very difficult game in its classical 8×8 format, it is not amenable to standard time performance assessments. The reason is that the input size is fixed, so we can't talk about the increase in running time as the size of the input grows. Since there are only finitely many configurations in the entire game — albeit a very large number of them — the winning-strategy problem for chess is a finite problem, and we can't really talk about its order-of-magnitude complexity.[15] We need inputs whose *size* is unlimited, like in Roadblock.

To make it possible to talk about the computational complexity of fixed-size board games, researchers define generalized versions,

---

[14] L. J. Stockmeyer and A. K. Chandra (1979). 'Provably Difficult Combinatorial Games', *SIAM J. Comput.* **8**, 151–74.

[15] We will discuss computerized chess in Chapter 7.

in which there is a different game for each board size. The N-game is played on an $N \times N$ board, and the set of pieces and allowed moves are generalized appropriately. There are natural ways to do this for chess and checkers, which we shall not describe here. What is interesting, however, is that the winning-strategy problems for generalized versions of both have been shown to be intractable too.[16]

problems that are even harder

All the examples of decidable but intractable problems that we have seen so far (the Towers of Hanoi, Roadblock, and generalized chess and checkers) have upper bounds of exponential time. In other words, they can all be solved in time 2^N or 3^N, or the like. Reality is a lot crueler: there are decidable problems that are much worse than that.

Consider a logical formalism, in which you can state things like 'if statement P is true then statement Q is false'. Suppose that we want the 'P's and 'Q's to be meaningful assertions about mathematical objects like the integers. For example, we might want to say something like 'if $X = 15$ then there is no Y such that $X = Y + Y$'. This statement happens to be true, since 15 is odd (and all values must remain integers). In the interests of trying to mechanize absolute mathematical truth, computer scientists seek efficient methods for determining the truth of such statements.

---

[16]A. S. Fraenkel and D. Lichtenstein (1981). 'Computing a Perfect Strategy for $n \times n$ Chess Requires Time Exponential in n', *J. Combinatorial Theory* **A31**, 199–214; J. M. Robson (1984). 'N by N Checkers is Exptime Complete', *SIAM J. Comput.* **13**, 252–67.

How hard is this particular truth-determination problem? Before addressing this question, we should explain double exponentials. Consider the function 2^{2^N}, which is 2 times itself, not N times, but 2^N Times. If N is a mere 5, the value of 2^{2^N} is over four billion, while if N is 7, the value is orders of magnitude larger than our friend the number of microseconds since the Big Bang. In fact, 2^{2^N} relates to the very bad function 2^N just as 2^N relates to the very good function N. It is therefore *doubly* bad.

Here are the facts regarding the problem of establishing the truth or fallacy of statements about the integers. Let us restrict the logic of integers so that the only arithmetic operations we are allowed to use in our statements is addition (the aforementioned statement about $X = 15$ is thus OK). More elaborate operations, such as multiplication or division, are forbidden. The resulting formalism, called **Presburger arithmetic,** has been shown to have double exponential-time upper and lower bounds. Any algorithm that can determine truth in this logic of integer addition — and there are such algorithms — is guaranteed to run for *horrendous* amounts of time on some very, very short statements.[17]

While truth in Presburger arithmetic is provably double exponential, another logical formalism for talking about arithmetic, with the cryptic name **WS1S**, is far worse. In this logic we can talk not only about the integers, but also about *sets* of integers, and all we need to allow here in way of operations is the addition of 1.

---

[17] M. J. Fischer and M. O. Rabin (1974). 'Super-Exponential Complexity of Presburger Arithmetic', in *Complexity of Computation* (R. M. Karp. ed.). Amer. Math. Soc., Providence, RI, pp. 27–41. The length N of an input formula in these logics is obtained by counting appearances of the arithmetical operations, '=', '+', and '×' (in the second case), and the logical operators like 'and', 'or', 'not', 'there exists', and so on.

That is, we can say things like 'there is a set of numbers S, every one of which has the property that if you add 1 to it then ...'. WS1S is unimaginably difficult to deal with algorithmically. Consider the *triple* exponential function $2^{2^{2^N}}$. To get a sense of how fast this function grows, if we were to plot it in the table given earlier, then on an input of size only 4, it would show the algorithm running for a 19 713-digit number of centuries (compare this with the 445-digit number for an N^N algorithm on an input of size 200). Can you fathom that?

So what's the story for WS1S? Well, first of all, WS1S is decidable. Algorithms have been devised to determine whether statements made within it are true or false. However, on the negative side, WS1S has been shown to admit no multiple exponential algorithm, for *any* multiple. This means that given any algorithm that is capable of determining truth in this logic, you can pile up as many 2s as you want in a cascade of exponentials of the form $2^{2^{2^{\cdots^N}}}$, and there will be formulas of length N that will require your algorithm to run for more than that amount of time![18] In such devastating cases, not only is the problem intractable, it is not even doubly, triply or quadruply intractable. We might simply say that, although in principle decidable, such a problem is highly intractable, or is of *unlimited* intractability.

If we take Presburger arithmetic, i.e. the ability to talk about integers, but relax the restriction on operations, allowing multiplication too, we get a formalism called **first-order arithmetic**. Interestingly, deciding truth in first-order arithmetic is undecidable!

---

[18] A. R. Meyer (1975). 'Weak Monadic Second Order Theory of Successor is not Elementary Recursive', in *Logic Colloquium* (R. Parikh, ed.), Lecture Notes in Mathematics, Vol. 453, Springer-Verlag, Berlin, pp. 132–154.

Even all the time in the world cannot help then.[19] Without wanting to make all this sound too depressing, if we combine the options in all of these logics, allowing the ability to talk about both integers and sets of integers, with the normal operations like addition and multiplication, we get **second-order arithmetic**, which is *highly* undecidable.[20]

We summarize the status of these four logics in the following table:

Logical formalism	Talks about	Time complexity
Presburger arithmetic	Integers with +	intractable (double exponential)
WS1S	Sets of integers with +	Highly intractable
First-order arithmetic	Integers with + and ×	Undecidable
Second-order arithmetic	Sets of integers with + and ×	Highly undecidable

unreasonable memory requirements

In the course of this chapter we concentrated on time performance, and we shall continue to do so in the next chapter. But before that we must spend a moment contemplating unreasonably bad consumption of memory space. There are algorithmic problems that have provable lower bounds of exponential space. This means

[19] K. Gödel (1931). 'Über formal unentscheidbare Sätze der Principia Mathematica und verwandter Systeme, I', *Monatshefte für Mathematik und Physik* **38**, 173–98.

[20] S. C. Kleene (1943). 'Recursive Predicates and Quantifiers', *Trans. Amer. Math. Soc.* **53**, 41–73.

that any algorithm solving them will require something like 2^N memory cells on certain inputs of size N.

This can have mind-boggling consequences. If a problem has a 2^N lower bound on memory space, then for any computer solving it (even if we were to build a special-purpose computer dedicated solely to that problem) there will be inputs of quite moderate size — less than 270, to be specific — that would require so much space for the intermediate steps of the computation, that even if each bit were the size of a *proton*, the whole known universe would not suffice to accommodate the machine!

Such unacceptably large resources are no joke. You just can't do it, regardless of money or brains, power or patience, race, color, age, or sex. This stuff is devastatingly bad, and the bad is for real.

chapter 4

sometimes we just don't know

Have you ever tried putting together a class schedule, pairing courses, time slots, and classrooms with teachers and instructors who have all kinds of constraints? Ever tackled a really hard jigsaw puzzle, full of look-alike pieces? Ever had to pack lots of bulky items of varying sizes and shapes into given boxes, trying to get them all in?

These are difficult tasks, you would have to admit. In carrying them out we seem to make local decisions one at a time, often reaching a dead end. If that happens, we backtrack a little, undo a recent decision and try something else instead. We then make some more progress, then backtrack again, maybe even further back than before, and so on. The entire process can take a long, long time.

These examples belong to a rich and diverse class of problems, many of which are of extreme importance in applications. Figuring out how hard they really are — specifically, whether or not they are tractable — is still wide open, and is one of the most profound and important unresolved questions in the world of computing.

the monkey puzzle

Let us start with a colorful example, not unlike the tiling problem of Chapter 2. A **monkey puzzle** involves nine square cards, whose sides depict the upper and lower halves of colored monkeys. The objective is to arrange the cards in a 3 × 3 square, such that wherever edges meet, the two monkey-halves match and the colors are identical (see Fig. 4.1).

Again, this is a puzzle, but cute puzzles are not our business. We are interested in the general algorithmic problem, of which the 3 × 3 monkey puzzle is but one small instance. The general problem receives as input the descriptions of N cards, where N is some square number. The output is a square arrangement of the N cards, if there is one, so that the colors and shapes match. Figure

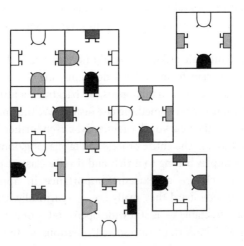

Fig. 4.1. The monkey puzzle.

4.1 shows an instance with $N = 9$.[1] In fact, we concentrate on the easier-looking yes/no version, which simply asks whether any such arrangement exists without asking for one to be exhibited.

A naïve solution comes immediately to mind. Since each input involves only a finite number of cards, and only finitely many locations are available for placing them, there are only finitely many different ways of arranging the cards into a square. And since it is easy to test the color-matching legality of any particular arrangement, an algorithm can be designed to work its way through *all* possible arrangements, testing each one in turn, and terminating with a 'Yes' if the arrangement at hand is legal (i.e. colors and monkey-halves match). If all possible arrangements have been considered, and have all been found to be illegal, the algorithm terminates and says 'No'.

Let us see what happens if the input is just slightly larger than the common 3×3 puzzle. Say N is 25, meaning that we are looking for 5×5 arrangements. How many candidate arrangements are there? Well, assuming we start at the bottom left-hand corner, there are 25 possible choices for the first card to be placed, and the particular card chosen can then be oriented in any of four possible directions. This gives 100 possibilities for the first 'move'. There are now 24 remaining cards, each of which can be placed in the second location and can also be oriented in four ways, yielding 96 possibilities for the second move. Since for each move made we must consider every possible choice of the next move, if we want to count possibilities, we must take the *product* of these two numbers, yielding a total of 9600 ways of carrying out the first two moves. By

---

[1] In contrast to the tiling problem, whose input consists of the *types* of tiles and a tiling can involve an unlimited supply of each type, here we are given the set of actual cards that have to be used.

the same reasoning, the third move can be carried out in $23 \times 4 = 92$ ways, which must be multiplied by the 9600, yielding 873 200 ways of making the first three moves. And so on. Continuing in this fashion, the total number of candidate arrangements of all 25 positions of the 5×5 square totals

$$(25 \times 4) \times (24 \times 4) \times (23 \times 4) \times \ldots \times (3 \times 4) \times (2 \times 4) \times (1 \times 4),$$

a number that can be written as $25! \times 4^{25}$. All of these will have to be checked by our naïve algorithm, one by one.

We shall not repeat the general properties of exponential functions that were discussed in Chapter 2. Still, it is worth reminding ourselves what this means: $25! \times 4^{25}$ is so amazingly large that a computer capable of checking a million arrangements per second (including all the bookkeeping involved) will take well over 533 *trillion trillion years* in the worst case to solve a single 25-card instance of the monkey puzzle! And recall that the Big Bang was a mere 12–15 billion years ago.

Thus, for the general N-card case, the worst-case running time of this naïve algorithm is proportional to $N! \times 4^N$, which is the product of two very nasty exponential functions. Of course, the algorithm can be designed more intelligently, but even the most sophisticated versions discovered to date are not that much better.[2]

---

[2] An improved version would operate in the backtrack fashion outlined above: put some card at the bottom left-hand corner; now try to find a card that fits above it, then one that fits to its right; and so on. At each stage, if no card from among those that are left fits, backtrack, by removing the last-positioned card and trying another in its place. This solution avoids the need to consider extensions of partial arrangements that have already been found to be illegal, and often dramatically cuts down on the total number of arrangements tested. In the worst case,

continued on next page

So, is that it, then? Is the problem really intractable, or does it admit some clever polynomial-time solution? Unfortunately, no-one knows the answer to this. The question is open.

NP-complete problems

You may feel that the monkey puzzle problem is amusing, but perhaps unworthy of further discussion. After all, isn't it just a puzzle?

Not at all. In truth, it is but one of hundreds and hundreds[3] of spectacularly diverse algorithmic problems, which, besides the monkey puzzle problem, include the ones mentioned in the opening paragraph of the chapter. They all exhibit precisely the same phenomena: they are decidable, but are not known to be tractable. They all admit exponential-time solutions, but for none of them has anyone ever found a polynomial-time algorithm. Moreover, no one has been able to prove that any of them require *super*-polynomial-time, and, in fact, the best known lower bounds for most of them are linear or quadratic. This means that it is conceivable (though unlikely) that they admit very efficient algorithms. We thus don't know what their inherent optimal solution is, and are faced with a disturbing algorithmic gap. The problems in this class are termed **NP-complete**, for reasons to be explained later.

---

continued
however, even this more efficient procedure will cause the inspection of almost all possible arrangements. The same thing happens if we try to recognize symmetric arrangements, or to use other such time-saving tricks; the numbers would be smaller, but in the worst case insignificantly so.

[3] The number is several thousand if you count less conservatively, labeling certain variants of the same problem as different.

The algorithmic gap associated with the NP-complete problems is enormous. The lower bounds we have for them are perfectly reasonable, so that if we found upper bounds (i.e. algorithms) to match, the problems would all be nicely and efficiently computable. However, the best upper bounds we have are devastatingly bad! The issue is not whether their running time is N, or $N\log_2 N$, or N^3, or whether we need 20 comparisons for a search or a million. Rather, it boils down to the ultimate question of whether or not we can ever hope to really solve these problems, even by the most powerful computers, with the very best software, programmed by the most talented people.

Are they good, these problems, or bad? The location of the NP-complete problems in the sphere of Fig 3.3 is thus unknown, since their upper and lower bounds lie on either side of the line dividing the tractable from the intractable. The question of where they actually reside surfaced in all its prominence in the early 1970s, following the work of Steven Cook, Leonid Levin, and Richard Karp, and is referred to as the **P vs. NP question**. It is still open, despite close to 30 years of intensive work by some of the best researchers in computer science.[4]

Two additional properties characterize the NP-complete problems, making their story all the more remarkable. One of the two

---

[4] S. A. Cook (1971). 'The Complexity of Theorem Proving Procedures', *Proc. 3rd ACM Symp. on Theory of Computing*, ACM, New York, pp. 151–8; L. A. Levin (1973). 'Universal Search Problems', *Problemy Peredaci Informacii* **9**, 115–16 (in Russian), English translation in *Problems of Information Transmission* **9**, 265–6; R. M. Karp (1972). 'Reducibility Among Combinatorial Problems', in *Complexity of Computer Computations* (R. E. Miller and J. W. Thatcher, eds.). Plenum Press, New York, pp. 85–104. See also M. R. Garey and D. S. Johnson (1979). *Computers and Intractability: A Guide to NP-Completeness*, W. H. Freeman & Co., San Francisco, CA.

is, in fact, quite astonishing. Before discussing them, however, we should see some more examples.

NP-complete problems abound in such scientific fields as combinatorics, operations research, economics, graph theory, game theory, and logic. They also arise daily in diverse real-world applications, ranging from telecommunication and banking to city planning and circuit design. As a result of this, and given the fundamental importance of separating the tractable from the intractable, the P vs. NP question has acquired a status unparalleled in the world of computing.

finding short paths

In the sample problems of Chapter 1 there are two that involve finding paths in road maps. Problem 6 asks for the shortest path between two given cities, *A* and *B*, and Problem 7, a decision problem, asks if there is a path whose total length is no more than some allowed bound, and which passes through all the cities in the map.

For easier comparison between them, let us modify these two problems as follows. We make the first a decision problem, to be more like the second, and add the two designated cities to the second, to be more like the first:

Problem 6′

Input: A road map of cities, with distances attached to road segments, two designated cities therein, *A* and *B*, and a number *K*.

Output: 'Yes' if it is possible to take a trip from *A* to *B* of length no greater than *K* miles, and 'No' if such a trip is impossible.

Problem 7′

Input: A road map of cities, with distances attached to road segments, two designated cities therein, *A* and *B*, and a number *K*.

Output: 'Yes' if it is possible to take a trip from *A* to *B*, which passes through all the cities and is of total length no greater than *K* miles, and 'No' if such a trip is impossible.

The inputs to the two problems are now identical, and the questions are very similar: in both cases we want to know whether or not there is a certain kind of short path between *A* and *B* (without asking for any output other than 'Yes' or 'No'), but Problem 7′ requires the path to 'visit' each of the cities. To illustrate Problem 7′, which is often called the **traveling salesman problem**, consider Fig. 4.2. It contains a seven-city road map, or network, in which the shortest tour from *A* to *B* that passes through all the other cities is of length 28. The answer should thus be 'Yes' if the bound *K* is, say, 30 or 28, and 'No' if it is 27 or 25. On the other hand, if

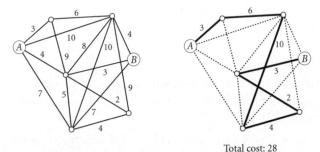

Total cost: 28

Fig. 4.2. The traveling salesman problem (not drawn to scale).

the input were to be exactly the same, but the question posed was that of Problem 6′, which is a yes/no version of the **shortest path problem**, the answer would be 'Yes' even with a bound of 25, since it is easy to find a path from A to B, not necessarily passing through all cities, whose length is less than that.

Neither of these problems is a toy example, and neither has to be about road maps and cities. They both arise in the design of communication systems and circuits, in planning construction lines and factory floors, and in the programming of industrial robots, to mention but a few applications. Shortest paths are crucial in planning real trips from place to place, in routing telephone calls and in network package transmission, for example. The traveling salesman problem is crucial in constructing newspaper distribution routes and the like, but it also occurs in an industrial setting. Suppose we are in the integrated circuit business, and we have to prepare a large number of identical circuit boards. As part of the task, we have a computerized drill that has to be programmed to drill, say, 200 holes in each board, at fixed locations. Clearly, since this has to be done many, many times, over and over again, it would be really nice if we could construct an optimal movement plan for the drill, starting at some point and making the trip through all locations. (Or, in the decision version, at least find out if this can be done within some limit of time or distance.)

Which of the two problems is harder, or are they roughly of the same complexity? In terms of the candidate paths that have to be taken into account, Problem 6′ — the shortest path problem — definitely seems to require more work. It has all possible paths from A to B to consider, whereas Problem 7′ — the traveling salesman problem — has to consider only the ones that pass through all the cities, and there are far fewer of those. The facts, however, are quite different, illustrating once again the shortcomings of simplistic intuition: the shortest path problem admits a fast algorithm (that runs in quadratic time, in fact), whereas the traveling salesman problem is NP-complete.

Recall what the latter fact implies: the traveling salesman problem is solvable, yes, but the only algorithms ever found for it are uselessly bad. (A straightforward one simply inspects all of the roughly $N!$ possible tours, for a map of N cities.) Even the best algorithms known for traveling salesmen (or saleswomen) are so bad as to be hopeless in the worst case for maps of 150 or 200 cities. And we must realize that while 150 cities might sound a lot to a traveling salesman with a suitcase full of bits and pieces, it is an extremely modest number for some of the real-world applications of the problem.

Its NP-completeness thus renders the traveling salesman problem unsolvable in practice — at least as far as our current knowledge goes.

scheduling and matching

Many NP-complete problems are concerned in one way or another with scheduling or matching. The class scheduling example mentioned earlier, sometimes called the **timetable problem**, is one. Say we are trying to get a new academic year set up in a high-school. Suppose we are given the availability of each teacher, the particular hours each of the classes can be scheduled, and the number of hours (possibly 0) that each of the teachers has to teach each of the classes. A satisfactory timetable is an assignment of teachers to classes to hours, so that all the given constraints are met, so that no two teachers teach the same class at the same time, and so that no two classes are taught by the same teacher at the same time. We don't even have to include other kinds of constraints, such as classroom size or student abilities, to make our point; things are bad enough even this way.

The timetable problem is NP-complete, as is the yes/no version that doesn't ask to exhibit a timetable, but wants to know only whether one exists.

Obviously, this problem is applicable to far more than just classroom scheduling. Teachers, time-slots, and classes can be replaced by pilots, aircraft, and missions, by FBI agents, motor-cycles, and crooks, by cars, garage lifts, and servicing procedures, or by computer tasks, processors, and system software routines.

Thus for timetable problems. As to matching, here too, many are NP-complete. They include fitting items into boxes or trucks (sometimes called the **bin-packing problem**), or assigning students to dormitories so that certain capacity requirements are satisfied.

It is not too difficult to come up with exponential-time algorithms for timetable and matching problems. They all have exponentially many candidate solutions, and an algorithm can be designed to carefully inspect them all. For example, all possible ways to schedule the teachers with the hours and the classes can be listed and checked, or all possible ways to pack the items into the boxes. Again, these naïve algorithms are hopelessly time-consuming, even for very reasonably sized inputs, since there are so many possibilities to check. And again, that these problems are NP-complete means that as of now no-one has been able to discover any substantially better way to solve them.

The fact that no good solution has been found for the timetable problem often raises eyebrows. Indeed there *are* software packages for this kind of thing, and people do use them. You don't hear complaints that they take zillions of years to run on the data of a local college or high-school. So what is going on? Well, the thing is that these 'solutions' compromise. Surprising as this may sound to their users, none of them is guaranteed to work in good (polynomial) time and to produce the right answer for each possible input situation. There will always be inputs, perhaps somewhat contrived, for which such software will either take far, far more time than we can afford to wait, or (and this is more common) it will overlook possibilities, stating that a particular set of constraints cannot be satisfied when in fact it can. A typical case would be for such a program to fail to find a constraint-satisfying timetable for a pilot/aircraft/mission instance of the problem, and to 'ask' for a couple of additional F-16s and a few more pilots, when it really could have done without them. Such software can be extremely helpful, and it very often discovers satisfactory timetables and matchings. However, in our present puristic setup, in which we require algorithms that are guaranteed to be always and absolutely correct, and to always terminate with the right answer within a polynomial amount of time, the timetable problem and the bin-packing problem and all their friends remain unsolved.

All this notwithstanding, there are many similar-looking scheduling and matching problems that *are* tractable. For example, if we have only two kinds of objects to fit into a timetable — say, teachers and hours, but with only one class to be taught, or hours and classes but with only one teacher — the problem does have good solutions.

more on puzzles

Getting back into the puzzle atmosphere, some of the most tantalizingly appealing NP-complete problems are based on two-dimensional arrangement tasks, like the monkey puzzle. Airlines used to hand out small kits containing a number of irregular shapes that had to be laid out to form a rectangle (see Fig. 4.3). You can buy these in many places, such as the gift-shops of science

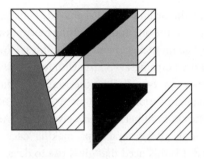

Fig. 4.3. An airline puzzle.

museums. The general decision problem that asks whether N such shapes can indeed form a rectangle is also NP-complete.

Now consider jigsaw puzzles. The standard kind, in which the picture is sufficiently heterogeneous, might be tedious to sit down and do by hand, but from a computational point of view it is not that hard; the work at each step is just a matter of running through all the unused pieces and finding the single one that fits. A non-fit can usually be detected by sight or when attempting to force the piece into place. The point is that backtracking is not really needed for such puzzles, a blessing that results in a quadratic time, perfectly reasonable algorithm.[5]

---

[5] Why quadratic time? Because when working on a heterogeneous jigsaw puzzle with N pieces in an orderly fashion from, say, the bottom left-hand corner, there are N possibilities for the first piece to place and four ways to place it; $N-1$ for the second piece and four ways to place it; $N-2$ for the third piece, etc. Since there is no backtracking to be done, you run through the $4N$ possibilities for the first move, find the one single piece that fits and that's that. Then through the $4(N-1)$ possibilities for the second move, find the one that fits and that's *that*. And so on. The total number of steps is thus the *sum* (not the product) of $4N$, $4(N-1)$, and so on, which is roughly $2N^2$.

So much for the ordinary, 'well-behaved', heterogeneous cases, where you look for the one and only fitting piece at each stage, find it, place it, and go on to bigger and better things. However, anyone who's ever labored on a jigsaw puzzle with lots of sky or sea knows that they are not that easy. Besides the confusion that comes from the homogeneous portions of the picture, many of the puzzle's pieces might be cut to fit perfectly in a given place. An error might be discovered only after several steps, making 'deep' backtracking necessary. And it is this need that gives rise to devastatingly time-consuming exponential time algorithms.

The general jigsaw problem, which has to cope with all possible input puzzles, including the really nasty ones, is also NP-complete. Thus, jigsaw puzzles, monkey puzzles, and airline arrangement puzzles are essentially all the same, and we shall see later that this 'sameness' is shared by *all* the NP-complete problems, not only those that are puzzle-like.

coloring networks

Here is another NP-complete problem, that involves coloring networks. Don't let its playful nature deceive you: this problem embodies the essence of several important applications. Further-more, in Chapter 6 we shall be turning its NP-completeness around, exploiting to our advantage the glum prospects of it ever becoming tractable.

The input is a network of points and lines, similar to a road map for the traveling salesman problem, but with no distances. Each point (or city) has to be colored, but in such a way that no two 'neighboring' points, that is, ones connected by a direct line, are colored the same. The problem asks for the minimal number of colors required to color a network. In the yes/no decision version, we are given a number K as an additional input, and simply have to say whether there is *any* way to K-**color** the input network (i.e. whether it can be colored using only K colors).

Figure 4.4 shows an example of a network colored legally with five colors. (We use shading and iconics to depict colors.) This particular network cannot be colored with less than that, so that if K is 5 or larger the answer should be 'Yes', but for 4 and below it is 'No'.

This problem, even in its yes/no guise, is NP-complete for any fixed K from 3 up. Thus, for input networks with something like 200 points, you can forget about being able to tell whether they can be colored with even a mere three colors.[6]

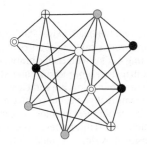

Fig. 4.4. Five-coloring a network.

---

[6] This problem is reminiscent of, but subtly different from, the famous **four-color question**, formulated in 1852 and considered to be one of the most interesting problems in all of mathematics. It went unsolved for over 120 years, and was finally settled in 1976. See K. I. Appel and W. Haken (1976). 'Every Planar Map is Four Colorable', *Bull. Amer. Math. Soc.* **82**, 711–12; T. L. Saaty and P. C. Kainen (1986). *The Four*

continued on next page

magic coins

It is now time to discuss the two additional properties of the NP-complete problems alluded to earlier. The first has to do with conviction and magic. Here is how it goes.

We know that it is apparently very, very difficult to figure out whether an NP-complete problem is to say 'Yes' or 'No' on a given input. But say you happen to know that the answer is 'Yes', and you are trying to convince someone of that fact. Interestingly, there is an easy way to do the convincing. For any NP-complete problem, each input has associated with it a so-called **certificate**, containing conclusive evidence to the effect that the answer on that input is 'Yes' if indeed it is 'Yes'. Moreover, this certificate is short — it is of

---

continued
Color Problem: Assaults and Conquest. Dover Publishers, New York. This mathematical problem involves coloring country maps, of the kind found in an atlas, by associating a color with each country, but in such a way that no two countries that share a border are colored with the same color. The question was whether four colors are sufficient to color *any* country map. At first sight, it seems that you could construct increasingly intricate maps, requiring ever-larger numbers of colors, as can be done for the problem of coloring networks. This, however, is not true, since countries reside in a two-dimensional world, and you can't have countries crawling under and over each other. In fact, the result proved in 1976 established that four colors indeed suffice. What is the connection with algorithmics? Since we now know that any country map can be colored with four colors, the *algorithmic* problem of determining whether a given input map can be 4-colored is trivial — simply output 'Yes' on all inputs. Not very interesting. For two colors, it is possible to show that a map is 2-colorable if, and only if, it contains no point that is at the junction of an odd number of countries. And since this property is easy to check, 2-colorability is not very interesting either. Three colors, however, *is* interesting: the problem of whether a country map can be 3-colored is NP-complete.

length that is polynomial in the size of the input in question — and can therefore be checked by the person you are trying to convince in an acceptable amount of time.

For example, it is notoriously difficult to tell whether a map of cities has a traveling salesman tour of length no more than a given number of miles. On the other hand, *if* such a path exists, it can be exhibited (as in Fig. 4.2) and easily checked by a doubtful party to satisfy the requirements. It thus serves as an excellent certification of the fact that the answer is 'Yes'. Similarly, although it is extremely difficult to satisfy the teachers/hours/classes constraints in the timetable problem, convincing someone that they *can* be satisfied (if you know that they can) is easy: simply exhibit a timetable. Checking that it satisfies the constraints, and thus justifying a 'Yes' answer, can be done in polynomial time. Likewise, exhibiting a legal arrangement of monkey puzzle cards provides an easily checkable certificate that the answer for this particular input is 'Yes'.

Thus, figuring out *whether* an NP-complete problem says 'Yes' to an input appears to be very hard, but certifying that it indeed does, *when* it does, is easy. Figuring out that an input yields a 'Yes' can be viewed as consisting of two parts: coming up with a candidate certificate, and checking that it is indeed a witnessing one. Checking is easy. Finding the certificate is the problematic part.

All this can be explained with magic. Let us assume that in solving some NP-complete problem we adopt the naïve approach of trying out all possibilities and backtracking when we get stuck. But say we have a special magic coin to help us out. Whenever a partial solution can be extended in more than one way (for example, several cards in the monkey puzzle can be legally placed in the current location, or the traveling salesman can proceed in one of several directions), the coin is flipped and the choice is made according to the outcome.[7] This coin, however, does not fall at random. It possesses magical insight, always indicating the best possibility: if one of the choices leads to a 'Yes', that is, to a full good solution, the magic coin points you there. If both possibilities lead to a 'Yes', or if none do, the coin acts like a normal random one, since it doesn't matter which way you go. The technical term used for such magic is **nondeterminism**; with it we no longer need a deterministic procedure to plow through all available options. We are guaranteed to reach the desired 'Yes' solution, if there is one.

As to the running time of such nondeterministic processes, it so happens that a little magic goes a long way. Although no-one knows whether the NP-complete problems are tractable, i.e. whether they can be solved properly (without magic) in a polynomial amount of time, what we *do* know is that every NP-complete problem has a polynomial-time *nondeterministic* algorithm. So magic — admittedly an imaginary resource — makes them all 'good'. This fact is intimately related to the existence of short certificates.[8]

We can now explain the cryptic acronym 'NP' in the term NP-completeness: it stands for *n*ondeterministic *p*olynomial-time: problems that become tractable when magic is allowed.

---

[7] If there are more than two possibilities, the coin is flipped several times.

[8] A short certificate can be gleaned directly from a polynomial-time 'magical' execution. To certify a 'Yes' answer, just follow the instructions of the magic coin and when the process terminates simply check whether it constructed a complete legal solution. Since the coin always indicates the best possibility, we can safely say 'No' if the solution is in violation of the rules. A legal solution would have been found by the coin if one existed.

standing or falling together

The final property of the NP-complete problems, and perhaps the most remarkable one, is their common fate. Either they are all tractable, or none of them is! The term 'complete' is used to signify this bind.

Let us sharpen this statement: if someone were to find a polynomial-time algorithm for any single NP-complete problem, thus establishing its tractability, there would immediately be polynomial-time algorithms for *all* of them. And this, in turn, implies the dual fact: if someone were to prove an exponential-time lower bound for any single NP-complete problem, thus establishing its *in*tractability, an immediate consequence would be that *no* such problem is tractable. In terms of Fig. 3.3, we don't know on which side of the tractable/intractable line the NP-complete problems really reside, but what we do know is that they are all either here or there *together*.

This is the ultimate in solidarity, and it is not a conjecture — it has been proved: all the NP-complete problems stand or fall together. We just don't know which way it goes. Paraphrasing again the brave old Duke of York,[9] we might say:

> *And when they are up they are up*
> *And when they are down they are down*
>
> *And since they can't be halfway up*
> *They are either up or down*

It is often difficult to see what causes such diverse problems to share their fate. But, in fact, they are all very closely related. A

---

[9] See W. S. Baring-Gould and C. Baring-Gould (1962). *Annotated Mother Goose*, Clarkson N. Potter, New York, p. 138.

criss-cross collection of **reductions** has been established between all the many NP-complete problems, establishing that if a polynomial time algorithm were ever found for any one of them it would transform immediately into an actual polynomial time algorithm for any other one.[10] If you find a good solution to the monkey puzzle problem, for example, then you immediately have amazingly good news for timetable preparers, traveling salesmen (and

---

[10] In practice, all you need to find in order to prove that a newly considered problem is NP-complete are two polynomial-time reductions: one *to* some already established NP-complete problem and one *from* such a problem. That such reductions exist between the new problem and *each* NP-complete problem then follows by the fact that a chain of polynomial time reductions is polynomial time too. For this reduction-finding to start somewhere, someone had to find a 'first' problem, and establish its NP-completeness by direct means. This was done in 1971 by Steven A. Cook in 'The Complexity of Theorem Proving Procedures', *Proc. 3rd ACM Symp. on Theory of Computing*, ACM, New York, 151–8 (1971), and around the same time by Leonid A. Levin, independently, in 'Universal Search Problems', *Problemy Peredaci Informacii* **9**, 115–16 (1973)(in Russian), or *Problems of Information Transmission* **9**, 265–6. They proved that determining truth in the simple logical formalism, called the **propositional calculus**, was NP-complete. In this logic, the abstract propositions, the '*F*'s and '*G*'s below can be combined to form more complex statements, using simple logical connectives such as 'and', 'or', 'not' and 'implies'. Thus, for example, the statement

not (*F* implies *G*) and (*G* or (*E* implies not *F*))

states that it is not the case that the truth of *E* implies the truth of *G*, and, besides that, either *G* is true or the truth of *E* implies that *F* is false. The algorithmic problem calls for determining whether an input statement is **satisfiable**, i.e. whether 'true's and 'false's can be assigned to the basic symbols so that the whole statement becomes true. The Cook/Levin theorem is considered to be one of the most important results in the theory of algorithmic complexity.

saleswomen), bin-packers, etc. And vice versa: if you manage to prove that the monkey puzzle does *not* have a polynomial-time solution, you can inform all these people that what they thought is bad news, really *is* bad news. It will then not be just that we haven't yet managed to find good solutions to their problems; we will know for sure that there aren't any such solutions to be found. The waiting and the hoping can end. The optimists will have lost. Just like that.

the great mystery: is P equal to NP?

The classes of problems we have been discussing have been given technical names by computer scientists. **PTIME**, or sometimes simply **P**, denotes what we have been calling the good, or tractable, problems; namely, those that admit polynomial-time algorithms. **NP** (without the 'complete') denotes the class of problems that admit magical, nondeterministic polynomial-time algorithms. The **NP-complete** problems are the 'hardest' problems in NP, in the stand-or-fall-together sense: if one of them turns out to be in P then all the problems that are in NP are also in P. Using these names, the profound unsolved question really boils down to whether or not P, as a class of problems, is equal to NP.

The P vs. NP question has been open since it was identified by Cook and Levin in 1971, and is one of the most difficult unresolved problems in computer science. It is definitely the most intriguing and the most important. Either all of these interesting and critically useful problems can be solved well by computer, or none of them can. Furthermore, you need only figure out the status of *one* of them to have put the entire issue at rest. Enormous research efforts have been made in trying to solve this problem, but to no avail. Most researchers believe that P ≠ NP, meaning that the NP-complete problems are inherently *in*tractable, but no one knows for sure. In any case, showing that an algorithmic problem is NP-complete is regarded as weighty evidence of its apparent intractability. Lacking proofs of true intractability for many problems, a proof of NP-completeness is the next best thing (or should we say the next *worse* thing).

Some problems are known to be *in* NP, i.e. they have fast magical solutions and short witnessing certificates, but are not known to be NP-complete. That is, we do not know whether they are among the select class of *hardest* problems in NP; we don't know if their fate is so intimately linked with timetables, traveling salesmen, and monkey puzzles. A well-known example involves testing a number for primality, Problem 3 in the list of Chapter 1. Despite the fact that no one has been able to find a polynomial-time algorithm for this, and despite the fact that primes have been shown to admit short certificates, i.e. the problem has a fast magical solution and thus is in NP,[11] it is not known to be NP-complete.

---

[11] V. R. Pratt (1975). 'Every Prime has a Succinct Certificate', *SIAM J. Comput.* 4, 214–20. Recall that the *length* of the input number K is what counts — i.e. the number of digits needed to write it down — not its value. If we were to use the *value* to determine time-complexity, then the simple primality test that runs through all odd numbers between 3 and the square root of K would be fine, since it takes time that is polynomial in K. However, the running time is exponential in K's *length*. We discuss this in more detail in Chapter 5.

can we come close?

Many of the NP-complete problems we have discussed are yes/no versions of **optimization problems**, in which we are interested in minimizing or maximizing something. The traveling salesman problem is a good example. Its original version asks for an optimal tour of all cities in the road map, that is, a tour of minimal length.

Now, although we don't know how to find the *best* tour, it is conceivable that we can find one that is not too much longer. In other words, we might be able to solve the problem in a way that is less than perfect, yet still of considerable practical value. Algorithms designed for this purpose are called **approximation algorithms**, and they are based on the assumption that taking a less-than-optimal tour is better than staying home, and finding a timetable with a few constraint violations is better than having total chaos.

One type of approximation algorithm produces results that are guaranteed to be not too far from the optimal solution. For example, there is a rather clever approximation algorithm for the traveling salesman problem, that runs in cubic time (that is, time N^3) and produces a tour guaranteed to be no longer than $1\frac{1}{2}$ times the (unknown) optimal tour.

Another type of approximation yields solutions that are not guaranteed to be always close to the optimum, but, rather, to be very close to the optimum *almost* always. For example, there is a fast algorithm for the traveling salesman problem that for some input road maps might yield tours much longer than the optimum, but in the vast majority of cases it yields almost optimal tours.

Do NP-complete problems always admit fast approximation algorithms? That is, if we are willing to be slightly flexible in our requirements for optimality, can we be sure to succeed? Well, this is a difficult question. People had harbored hopes that powerful approximation algorithms could be found for most NP-complete problems even without knowing the answer to the real P vs. NP question. The hope was that we may be able to come *close* to the optimal result even though finding the *true* optimum would still be beyond our reach. Recently, however, this hope has been delivered a crippling blow with the discovery of more bad news: for many NP-complete problems (not all), approximations turn out to be no easier than full solutions! Finding a good approximation algorithm for any one of these problems has been shown to be tantamount to finding a good non-approximate solution. Flexibility will take you nowhere you couldn't already have gone in full rigidity.[12]

This has the following striking consequence. Finding a good *approximation* algorithm for one of these special NP-complete problems is enough to render *all* the NP-complete problems truly tractable; that is, it would establish that P = NP. Put the other way around, if P ≠ NP, then not only do the NP-complete problems have no good *full* solutions, but many of them can't even be approximated!

As an example, consider the network coloring problem. Since finding the smallest number of colors needed to color a given network is NP-complete, researchers looked for an approximation algorithm that would come close to the optimal number in a good, i.e. polynomial, amount of time. So perhaps there is a method,

---

[12] U. Feige, S. Goldwasser, L. Lovász, S. Safra, and M. Szegedy (1996). 'Approximating clique is almost NP-complete', *J. Assoc. Comput. Mach.* **43**, 268–92; S. Arora and S. Safra (1996). 'Probabilistic Checkable Proofs: A New Characterization of NP', *J. Assoc. Comput. Mach.* **45**, 70–122; S. Arora, C. Lund, R. Motwani, M. Sudan and M. Szegedy (1998). 'Proof Verification and Intractability of Approximation Problems', *J. Assoc. Comput. Mach.* **45**, 501–55.

which, given an input network, finds a number that is never more than 10% or 20% larger than the minimal number of colors needed to color the network. Well, it turns out that even for 50% this is as hard as the real thing: researchers have recently proved that if any polynomial-time algorithm can find a coloring with no more than twice the minimal number of colors needed to color a network, then there is a polynomial-time algorithm for the original problem of finding the optimal number itself.[13] This has the far-reaching ramifications just explained: discovering a good approximation algorithm for coloring networks is just as difficult as showing that P = NP. So there goes the hope for that.

sometimes we succeed

The P vs. NP question is one of many unknowns in the theory of algorithmic complexity — perhaps the most significant one. But there are many others too. For example, it is not known whether reasonable space is any different from reasonable time: is there a problem solvable with a polynomial amount of memory space that cannot be solved in polynomial-time? This is the P vs. PSPACE question. In fact, NP, the class of problems solvable in polynomial-time with magical nondeterminism, lies between PTIME and PSPACE, but no-one knows whether it is equal to one or the other, or whether all three are distinct.

This does not mean that we are not treated once in a while to spectacular good news. Sometimes a polynomial-time algorithm is found for a problem whose tractability/intractability status was unknown. An important example is linear planning, better known

---

[13] C. Lund and M. Yannakakis (1994). 'On the Hardness of Approximating Minimization Problems', *J. Assoc. Comput. Mach.* 41(5), 960–81.

as **linear programming**. This is a general framework that encompasses certain kinds of planning problems where time and resource constraints have to be met in a cost-efficient way. The linear planning problem, it must be emphasized, is *not* NP-complete, but the best solution anyone was able to find for it was a well-known exponential-time algorithm called the **simplex method**, invented in 1947 by G. B. Dantzig.[14] This algorithm, by the way, is not all that bad: despite the fact that certain inputs force it to run for an exponential amount of time, they are rather contrived, and tend not to arise in practice. When used for most real problems of realistic size, the simplex method performs very well. Nevertheless, the problem was not known to be tractable in the strict sense of the word, nor was there a lower bound to show that it wasn't.

In 1979, a rather ingenious polynomial-time algorithm was found for the problem, but it was something of a disappointment. The exponential-time simplex method outperformed it in many of the cases arising in practice. Nevertheless, it did show that linear programming is in P. Recent work based on this algorithm has produced more efficient versions, and people currently believe that before long there will be a fast polynomial-time algorithm for linear planning that will be useful in practice for all inputs of reasonable size.[15]

* * *

[14] G. B. Dantzig (1963). *Linear Programming and Extensions*. Princeton University Press, Princeton, NJ.

[15] L. G. Khachiyan (1979). 'A Polynomial Algorithm in Linear Programming', *Doklady Akademiia Nauk SSSR* **244**, 1093–6 (in Russian), English translation in *Soviet Mathematics Doklad* **20**, 191–4; N. Karmarkar (1984). 'A New Polynomial-Time Algorithm for Linear Programming', *Combinatorica* **4**, 373–95.

In Chapters 2 and 3 we discussed algorithmic problems that we know to be unsolvable, and others that we know cannot be solved in practice. Obviously, these will not bring us any joy. Nor is there comfort in the problems of this chapter, for which we don't know whether we should laugh or cry: they appear to be bad, are conjectured by many to be bad, but we don't know for sure.

But what about the everyday? Is it true that most problems arising in common applications *can* be solved efficiently? Unfortunately, the answer is no. Not at all. It's just that we often tend to equate 'everyday' and 'common' with situations that we know how to tackle. In actuality, a growing number of problems arising in real applications turn out to be NP-complete or worse, and for some of these we can't even resort to approximation algorithms.

Bad news. Bad news indeed.

chapter 5

trying to ease the pain

The fact that computing doesn't bring only good news has pushed researchers in a number of directions, intended to try to alleviate the problem. In this chapter we shall discuss some of the most interesting of these: **parallelism** (or **concurrency**), **randomization**, **quantum computing**, and **molecular computing**. Each of the first two represents a new algorithmic paradigm by relaxing a fundamental assumption underlying conventional computing. The third transfers computation into the mysterious realm of quantum mechanics, and the fourth represents an attempt to have molecules do the work.

To get a feeling for parallelism, consider the following. Several years ago there was a contest in the Los Angeles area for the world title in fast house building. Certain rigid rules had to be adhered to, involving things like the number of rooms, the utilities required, and allowed building materials. No prefabrication was permitted, but the foundations could be prepared ahead of time. A house was deemed finished when people could literally start living in it; all plumbing and electricity had to be in place and functioning perfectly, trees and grass had to adorn the yard, and so on. No limit was placed on the size of the building team.

The winning company used a team of about 200 builders, and had the house ready in a little over *four hours*!

This is a striking illustration of the benefits of parallelism: a single person working alone would need a lot more time to complete the house. It was only by working together, amid incredible feats of cooperation, coordination, and mutual effort, that the task could be accomplished in so short a time. Parallel computation allows many computers, or many processors within a single computer, to work on a problem together, in parallel.

As to randomization, Russian roulette is a good illustration. While some people might consider unlikely the chances of getting killed in playing this 'game', most people would not and would never agree to participate. Fine. But let's now suppose that instead of a mere six bullet positions, the revolver has 2^{200} of them. A simple calculation shows that, in terms of risk, this is the same as saying that the trigger in an ordinary six-bullet revolver is actually pulled only if the single bullet always end up in the shooting position in 77 consecutive spins. The chances of getting killed in a 77-spin game are many, many orders of magnitude smaller than the chances of achieving the same effect by drinking a glass of water, driving to work or taking a deep breath of air. If you have some important reason to participate in a 2^{200}-position or 77-spin game, then you have absolutely no reason to worry about the risk involved; the probability of a catastrophe is unimaginably minute.

In line with this example, randomization allows algorithms to toss fair coins (or spin revolver barrels, if you will) in the course of their action, yielding random outcomes. The consequences are surprising. Rather than introducing chaotic and unpredictable results, we shall see that this new ability can be extremely useful. It often yields fast randomized, or probabilistic, solutions to problems for which the only conventional solutions known are far less efficient. The price paid is the possibility of error, but, as in the roulette scenario, this possibility can be safely ignored.

Quantum computing is a brand new approach to computation, based on quantum mechanics, that tantalizing and paradoxical piece of 20th century physics. So far, a few surprisingly efficient quantum algorithms have been discovered for problems not known to be tractable in the 'classical' sense. However, to work they require the construction of a special **quantum computer**, something that as of now is still very much nonexistent. Molecular, or DNA computing, another very recent paradigm, has enabled researchers to coax a molecular solvent to solve instances of certain NP-complete problems, which raises interesting and exciting possibilities.

The rest of the chapter discusses these ideas in varying levels of detail. However, being true to our goal of presenting bad news, we shall concentrate on whether even these more liberal ways of solving algorithmic problems are able to overcome the inherent limitations discussed in the previous chapters.

parallelism, or joining forces

The house-building story makes it clear that doing many things in parallel can work wonders. Still, it's important to realize that you can't parallelize just anything. Consider digging a ditch, one foot deep, one foot wide, and ten feet long, and assume that a single person can dig a cubic-foot hole in an hour. A single digger would need ten hours to dig a ten foot ditch, but ten people could do the job in one hour by working concurrently, side by side. Parallelism is at its best here. But say that we want a *well*, not a ditch, and a well is one foot wide, one foot long, and ten feet *deep*. Here parallelism achieves nothing, and even a hundred people would need ten hours to get the job done.

A similar example involves nine couples trying to join forces in having a child in one month ....

Some algorithmic problems *can* be nicely 'parallelized', despite the fact that the first solutions that come to mind are sequential in nature.[1] Consider the salary summation problem of Chapter 1. It might appear necessary to do what we did, namely, to run through the list of employees linearly, adding the salaries one at a time; just like digging a well. Not so. Figure 5.1 illustrates a simple parallel algorithm for salary summation that runs in logarithmic time — a momentous improvement over linear time, as shown in Chapter 3. The method is to first consider the entire list of N employees two by two, in pairs;

$$<1^{st}, 2^{nd}>, <3^{rd}, 4^{th}>, <5^{th}, 6^{th}>\dots,$$

and to sum the two salaries in all pairs *simultaneously*, yielding a list of half the length of the original. This takes the time of a single addition only, since all $N/2$ summations of the pairs are carried out at the same time. The new list (of length $N/2$) is then arranged similarly in pairs, and the two numbers in each pair are again added simultaneously, yielding a new list of $N/4$ numbers. This continues until there is only one number left, which is the sum of

---

[1] The term **sequential processing** is usually used to contrast with parallel processing, and denotes the usual way of computing with a single computer, or processor.

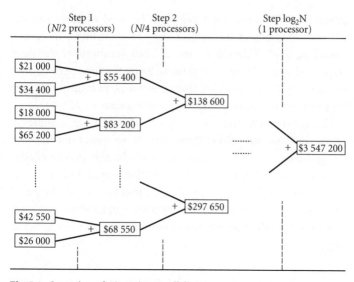

Fig. 5.1. Summing salaries using parallelism.

the salaries in the entire list. The total number of steps this takes is the logarithm base 2 of N, so the entire logarithm runs in time proportional to log N.

With the table of Chapter 3 in mind, this logarithmic running time means that 1000 salaries can summed in the time that it takes to carry out just 10 additions, and a million salaries can be summed in the time of only 20 additions. Great savings indeed.

But we should also talk about the hardware required for this, namely, the number of processors we would need. This complexity measure is sometimes termed **hardware size**. To simultaneously carry out the half million additions of two salaries required in the first step of summing a million salaries, we need half a million processors. The same ones can then be used to carry out the 250 000 additions of the second stage (half of them, of course, would be idle), followed by the 125 000 additions of the third stage, and so on. In general, then, to bring the time performance of summing N salaries down from linear time to logarithmic time we need $N/2$ processors, a number that depends on N.

This is necessarily the case, for if we only had a *fixed* number of processors, one that didn't grow with N, we could not improve things beyond a constant factor: we might be able to sum salaries twice as fast, or 100 times as fast, but the overall time performance would still be proportional to N, that is, it would be linear time. To achieve an order-of-magnitude improvement requires **expanding parallelism**, where the number of processors grows as N grows.[2]

can parallelism eliminate the bad news?

So parallelism can improve things: many problems can be solved faster, even in order-of-magnitude terms, if parallelism is allowed.

---

[2] You might conceivably claim that a growing number of processors is just not feasible, since computers are of fixed size. In a puristic sense this is true, but a similar argument could be made about memory space, and perhaps also about time. The purpose of complexity measures is to provide means for estimating how the amount of resources grows as inputs get larger. We must be able to solve an algorithmic problem for tomorrow's inputs too, without having to come up with a new algorithm each time. In this respect, processors are considered a resource as any other, and we want to know how large the hardware has to be for ever-larger inputs.

Not all problems, of course, but some. Digging ditches yes, but digging wells no. You can feed nine babies fast with nine pairs of parents, but you can't produce one baby faster than the norm, even with such a team.

Good. So can we put all this bad news nonsense aside now?

Let's see. The first thing to ask is whether parallelism can solve problems that could not have been solved at all otherwise. Can we devise a parallel algorithm for a noncomputable or undecidable problem? The answer is no. Any parallel algorithm can be simulated sequentially, by a single processor that runs around doing everyone's work. This will typically take much longer than the parallel algorithm, but it can be done. An immediate consequence is that the Church–Turing thesis applies to parallel models of computation too: the class of problems solvable by algorithmic devices is insensitive even to the addition of parallelism. Even harnessing all the world's computers in a mighty universal effort would not solve the tiling problem or enable us to detect Y2K bugs. So much for that.

The next question is whether parallelism can turn intractable problems into tractable ones. Is there a problem requiring an unacceptable (that is, super-polynomial) amount of time for *sequential* solution that can be solved in *parallel* in acceptable (that is, polynomial) time?

To be able to better appreciate the subtlety of this question, consider the NP problems of Chapter 4. As you may recall, all problems in NP have good nondeterministic solutions. They can be solved efficiently with the aid of a magic coin, which, if tossed when confronted with a choice, will use its wizardry to point in the direction that leads to the best answer — a 'Yes' for a decision problem — if there is such a direction. Now here is the interesting fact: if we have parallelism we don't need the magic coin. Whenever a 'crossroad' is reached, lacking magic we simply send off new processors to follow all the possibilities simultaneously. If one of them ever comes back and says 'Yes', the entire process halts and says 'Yes' too; if a predetermined polynomial amount of time has elapsed and none of them has said 'Yes', the process halts and says 'No'. The fact that the problem is in NP means that a 'Yes' answer (if the answer is indeed 'Yes') would have been discovered using a magic coin in this amount of time, so that our exhaustive, multiple-processor traversal of all possibilities will find the 'Yes' in the same amount of time too. If it doesn't find a 'Yes' within the allotted time, the answer must be 'No'.

Consequently, all problems in NP, including the NP-complete ones, such as monkey puzzles, traveling salesmen, timetables, and box-packing, have polynomial-time parallel solutions.

Neat. So, is this not intractability made tractable?

Well, no, not quite. Two comments are in order, before we rush off telling everyone that intractability is but a bothersome consequence of old-fashioned one-processor computing, and that it can be eliminated by using parallelism.

First, we only know how to make NP-complete problems good: but we don't know how to do so for the *provably* bad ones (like Roadblock; for example). None of the NP-complete problems is known to be intractable — they are merely conjectured to be so. Thus, the fact that we can solve NP-complete problems in polynomial time using parallelism doesn't imply that parallelism can rid even a single problem of its inherent intractability, since we don't know whether the NP-complete problems are *really* intractable.

Second, and more importantly, the hardware size needed for carrying out a good parallel algorithm will very often be bad! In particular, this is true for the above method for solving NP-complete problems: if we try to avoid the need for a magic coin by parallel consideration of all possibilities, we are in for a big surprise. Exponentially big, in fact! Using parallelism to figure out in less than zillions and zillions and zillions of years whether class schedules can be found that satisfy the constraints of high schools, you would need a wholly unreasonable computer containing zillions and zillions and zillions of intricately connected processors. Moreover, even though the parallel algorithm has a polynomial time bound, it is by no means obvious that it can actually be run in polynomial time on a real parallel computer. Researchers have proved that under quite liberal assumptions about the width of communication lines and the speed of communication, a super-polynomial number of processors would often require a super-polynomial amount of actual time to carry out even a *polynomial* number of steps, no matter how the processors are packed together. These results are based on the inherent limitations of three-dimensional space.[3] Put more concisely, good parallel time often comes with the unwanted guest of extremely bad hardware size, and moreover, this good time doesn't necessarily stay good when the hardware is bad.

The question thus remains: can we use parallelism, even with unreasonably sized hardware, to solve in an acceptable amount of time a problem that is provably unsolvable sequentially in an acceptable amount of time? This question is still open, leaving a

---

[3] P. M. B. Vitànyi (1988). 'Locality, Communication and Interconnect Length in Multicomputers', *SIAM J. Comput.* 17, 659–72.

big gap in our understanding of what can really be achieved by entities working together.[4]

---

[4] Interestingly, **parallel-PTIME** (problems solvable in polynomial-time using parallelism) turns out to be equivalent to the class PSPACE (problems solvable sequentially using a polynomial amount of memory space). Therefore, the question of whether parallel-PTIME is strictly larger than PTIME is really equivalent to a question involving sequential computation only, namely, whether PSPACE is strictly larger than PTIME. This P vs. PSPACE question is considered by researchers to be very difficult, and not unlike the P vs. NP question of Chapter 4. Another central question that arises is what we really mean when we refer to 'good' in the presence of parallelism. Parallel PTIME might not be the right choice, since, as mentioned, polynomial time parallel algorithms may require an exponential number of processors, and may take more than a polynomial amount of time to run on a real parallel machine. Also, one of the purposes of introducing parallelism is to *reduce* running time, drastically if possible. We often want *sublinear* algorithms, that exploit parallelism to such an extent that they don't even have to read the entire input in order to do their work. An interesting response to this challenge involves a class of problems called NC, defined as those that admit *extremely* fast parallel solutions, much faster even than linear time (poly-logarithmic time, in fact), and require only polynomially many processors. See N. Pippenger (1979). 'On Simultaneous Resource Bounds (preliminary version)', *Proc. 20th IEEE Symp. On Foundations of Computer Science.* IEEE, New York, pp. 307–11; S. A. Cook (1981). 'Towards a Complexity Theory of Synchronous Parallel Computation', *L'Enseignement Mathèmatique* 27, 99–124. Although many problems, such as sorting, turn out to be in NC, there are still many things we don't know about this class. For example, no-one knows whether this kind of speedup is possible for *all* problems in PTIME. Thus, while it is known that NC is contained in PTIME — which, in turn, is contained in NP, which, in turn, is contained in PSPACE — it is not known whether these three inclusions are *strict*, but many computer scientists believe that they are. The situation is thus as follows, where the symbol $\overset{?}{\subset}$ means 'is a smaller set than, but is not known to be *strictly* smaller than':

$$\text{NC} \overset{?}{\subset} \text{PTIME} \overset{?}{\subset} \text{NP} \overset{?}{\subset} \text{PSPACE} \ (= \text{parallel-PTIME})$$

continued on next page

But there is more to research in this area than trying to solve such as-of-now unyielding open questions. Parallelism, or concurrency, is a fact of life, and the better we understand it the more we can use it to our advantage. As it stands, recent algorithmic and technological advances in this area seem to be ahead of each other. Many of the best parallel algorithms devised cannot be implemented because existing parallel computers are inadequate in some way or another. In fact, very few parallel algorithms have ever been run effectively on real parallel computers, and this includes some of the fastest ones invented. On the other hand, we still don't have a good enough understanding of what can be algorithmically parallelized to take full advantage of the features those same computers offer.

randomization, or tossing coins

Parallelism landed us outside the world of conventional algorithms, in that it allowed the utilization of more than one processor. This

---

continued

Put in words, the conjectures (from right to left) are as follows: (i) There are problems that can be solved sequentially with a good amount of memory space — which is the same as being solvable in parallel in good time (but possibly bad hardware size) — that cannot be solved sequentially in good time even with magical nondeterminism. (ii) There are problems that can be solved sequentially in good time with magical nondeterminism that cannot be solved sequentially in good time without it. (iii) There are problems that can be solved sequentially in good time that cannot be solved in parallel in extremely little time with good hardware size. These are three of the deepest, most important and most difficult open questions in computer science. Proving or disproving any one of them would constitute a major breakthrough in understanding the true fundamentals of computation.

new freedom is easily seen to improve things, and required little justification. We now extend conventional computing in a totally different way, by allowing algorithms to toss coins during their execution, yielding random outcomes. Such algorithms are termed probabilistic, or randomized.

Computers tossing coins?! Doesn't that introduce chaotic, unpredictable behavior into the otherwise orderly, carefully specified, step-by-step world of algorithmic processing? Well, yes it does, but in many cases we can *exploit* the unpredictability of tossing a coin, making it work *for* us instead of against us. There are basically two ways to do this. In the first, dubbed the **Las Vegas** approach,[5] a correct but inefficient algorithm is constructed, and randomness is used to help expedite its execution with high probability. In a nutshell, Las Vegas algorithms are characterized by being always correct and probably fast.

An example involves **quicksort**, a very popular sorting algorithm. Quicksort happens to have a rather disappointing worst case running time (N^2, which for sorting is slow — see Chapter 3), but a very good average case one, namely about $1.5 \times N \log_2 N$, which often makes it the sorting algorithm of choice. However, certain applications give rise to uneven collections of input lists that cause quicksort to perform badly, closer to the quadratic worst-case bound. Curiously, if the input list is already sorted, and thus requires no work at all, the algorithm will not detect this fact and will perform its absolute worst, running in quadratic time! What can be done about this, to cause inputs to act like average

---

[5] The terms 'Las Vegas' and 'Monte Carlo' are not particularly telling, but for some reason they are the ones used by computer scientists, and they seem to have stuck.

trying to ease the pain   131

ones? Simple: we will first shake up the input in an arbitrary fashion. More precisely, we carry out a preprocessing stage prior to applying the quicksort procedure itself, in which coin tossing is used to shuffle up the input list according to a random permutation. This guarantees that the list sent off to be sorted will be an 'average' list. Far from making things any worse, this strange trick causes the running time, with high probability, to be much closer to the excellent average case bound. The resulting 'mix-and-then-sort' algorithm is of the Las Vegas type. It always sorts correctly and is very fast with high probability. With some small probability it could run in the not-so-good time of N^2.

The other kind of randomized algorithm is termed **Monte Carlo**. This approach takes a far more radical leap, renouncing our most sacred requisite, namely, that a solution to an algorithmic problem must solve that problem correctly for all possible inputs. Of course, we can't abandon correctness completely, since then any algorithm would 'solve' any problem. Nor do we recommend that people use algorithms that they *hope* will work, but whose performance they can only speculate about, and not analyze. Rather, we are interested in algorithms that might not *always* be correct, but whose possible incorrectness is something that can be safely ignored. And we insist that this fact be justifiable on rigorous mathematical grounds. In contrast to Las Vegas algorithms, which are always correct, and probably fast, Monte Carlo algorithms are always fast, but are only probably correct. The probability, however, must be very, very high.

Here is an example. Suppose you are organizing a large dinner party where the guests are to bring the food. But you want some order. Instead of each guest bringing whatever they want, you would like about a quarter of them to bring appetizers, about a half to bring main courses, and the remaining quarter to bring desserts. (You provide the wine and beer.) A naïve way to arrange this is for you to determine the assignments yourself, according to your quarter/half/quarter scheme. A randomized approach, which is easier for you (because you don't have to keep track of who was told what and you avoid the inevitable arguments with people about their assignments), is as follows. Simply tell each guest to toss a coin at home. If the outcome is 'Heads', they bring a main course, otherwise they toss again. If the outcome on the second throw is 'Heads', they bring an appetizer, and if it is 'Tails' they bring a dessert. With very high probability (that gets higher as the dinner party gets larger), the food will be as you wanted. Not always, and not exactly, but it will come very close most of the time.

more on Monte Carlo algorithms

Randomized algorithms are used for things far more critical than making sure you're not stuck with a table full of appetizers.

Consider the following situation, which is not unlike the Russian roulette story discussed earlier, but involves money rather than lives. Assume that, for some reason, all your money was tied up to the monkey puzzle problem of Chapter 4 in the following way. You are given a single large instance of the problem (say a 15×15 version with 225 cards), and are told that your money will be doubled if you can say correctly whether the cards can be arranged in a legal 15×15 square. You are also told that you lose the lot if you give the wrong answer. To discourage indecision, the money is unavailable until you give *some* answer. Since the monkey puzzle problem is NP-complete, you have a real problem. What do you do?

You could run your favorite exponential-time monkey puzzle algorithm on the input cards, hoping that this particular case is an easy one and will be solved reasonably fast, or you could position yourself on the floor and start trying things out on your own. Alternatively, realizing that these options are useless, you might simply guess 'Yes' or 'No' and hope for the best. At least there you have a 50% chance of succeeding.

Is there any better way?

Suppose some kind soul approached you just as you were about to make your wild guess, and offered you (cheaply) a Monte Carlo algorithm that solved the monkey puzzle problem fast, but with a slight chance of error: it was guaranteed that it gave the wrong answer only once in every 2^{200} runs. Is that good news? It sure is. You money is as safe as any. Take the deal. Run this algorithm on the input cards and present your tormenter with the answer. As in the 2^{200}-position version of Russian roulette, the chances of losing your money are far, far less than the chances of a hardware error occurring in all the bank's computers together, precisely during this execution, or the chances of your bank going bankrupt anyway the very next day.

The fact is that for many algorithmic problems, including some that appear to be intractable, such extremely-small-probability-of-error algorithms exist, and are usually very time-efficient. Whether or not such solutions exist for the monkey puzzle problem or for other NP-complete problems is still not known, but for many similar problems they do. So our little scenario about your money is not yet doable with the monkey puzzle, but it is doable with other problems, such as the one described in the next section. For all conceivable practical purposes, a randomized algorithm of the Monte Carlo type is perfectly satisfactory, whether it is an individual's money or life that is at stake, a company's financial future, or an entire country's security. The chances of a mishap are negligible, and, as we shall see, *you* are the one who gets to determine ahead of time how large a risk you are willing to take.

testing for primality

An important utilization of randomization is in testing a number for primality. Problem 3 on the list of Chapter 1 was this:

Problem 3

Input: A positive integer K.
Output: 'Yes' if K is prime and 'No' if it isn't.

The primes constitute the most interesting class of numbers ever to have caught mathematicians' attention. They play a central role in the branch of mathematics known as **number theory** and have many remarkable properties. Their investigation has led to some of the most beautiful results in all of mathematics. Also, as we shall see in Chapter 6, prime numbers are fast becoming indispensable in several exciting applications of algorithmics, such as cryptography, where it is important to be able to quickly test the primality of large numbers.

How do we determine whether a number K is a prime? Chapter 1 mentioned the naïve method of dividing K by all the integers between 2 and $\sqrt{K}$. We pronounce K composite if any one of these potential divisors is found to divide it without a remainder, and decide that it is prime if all divisions have been carried out and have all yielded remainders. This algorithm is fine. It is simple, it is correct, and it works quite nicely for numbers of 20 digits or so. Unfortunately, many of the interesting applications require much larger primes — say, 150- or 200-digit ones. We have to know how the naïve algorithm behaves as K grows, and the number of digits is the right thing to be looking at, since in primality testing, as in most other number theoretic algorithmic problems, the size of the input is not the *value* of the numbers at hand but their *length* in digits. Thus, we would like to know just how fast this primality testing algorithm is as a function of N, the number of digits in the input number K.[6]

The sad fact is that even with the best improvements known, such as passing over multiples of candidate dividers that have already been tested, this common primality testing algorithm is unreasonably inefficient; its time complexity is exponential in N. On a 200-digit number it could take many, many billions of years using even the fastest computers. There are better algorithms than this, but they are still not polynomial time, and the problem is not known to be tractable in the usual sense.[7]

---

[6] The **basis** of the digital representation is unimportant here: there are only linear differences between the length of a number written in binary or in decimal representation, or in any other representation that utilizes at least two digits.

[7] In contrast to the NP-complete problems, there are many people who believe that primality testing *is* in PTIME. In fact, there are algorithms for primality testing that run in 'almost' polynomial time, at least in terms of order-of-magnitude complexity. The best one currently runs in time O $(N^{O(\log_2 \log_2 N)})$, which can be considered very close to polynomial time, since the function $\log_2 \log_2 N$ grows very slowly; the first N for which it exceeds 5 is more than four billion, and it doesn't reach 6 until N is well over 18 billion billion. See L. Adelman, C. Pomerance, and R. S. Rumely

continued on next page

randomized primality testing

This bleak news notwithstanding, in the mid-1970s, following early work of Michael Rabin on probabilistic computing, a couple of ingenious Monte Carlo algorithms were discovered for testing primality. They were among the first randomized solutions to be found for hard algorithmic problems, and have triggered extensive research that has led to improved solutions to many other problems too. The running times of these primality testing algorithms are (low-order) polynomials in the length N of input number K. They can test the primality of a 200-digit number with negligible probability of error remarkably fast on even a very small computer![8]

The algorithms are based on searching at random for a certain kind of certificate, or **witness**, to K's compositeness. Such a witness is a number whose special mathematical properties serve as a true proof of the fact that K is composite. If a witness is found, the algorithm can safely stop and say 'No, K is not prime', since it has acquired undisputable evidence of that fact. However, the setup

---

continued
(1983). 'On Distinguishing Prime Numbers from Composite Numbers', *Ann. Math.* **117**, 173–206. If we disregard constant factors for a moment, this means that on an input number with a billion digits — that is, a number K whose length N is a billion — the algorithm still runs within a time bound of roughly N^5, and K has to have over 18 billion billion digits before it starts behaving according to the bound of N^6. Nevertheless, this is still super-polynomial time performance, since eventually it *will* reach N^6, and then N^7, and so on, without limit.

[8] M. O. Rabin (1980). 'Probabilistic Algorithm for Testing Primality', *J. Number Theory* **12**, 128–38; G. L. Miller (1976). 'Riemann's Hypothesis and Tests for Primality', *J. Comput. Syst. Sci.* **13**, 300–17; R. Solovay and V. Strassen (1977). 'A Fast Monte-Carlo Test for Primality', *SIAM J. Comput.* **6**, 84–5.

must be such that at some reasonably early point in time the algorithm will be able to stop searching and declare that K is prime, with a very small chance of being wrong.

To help appreciate the difficulty of defining such witnesses, let's see what happens if we try to work with the obvious candidates, namely, K's factors. Say we define a witness to be any number between 2 and $K - 1$ that divides K exactly. We now go ahead trying to find such a number by random guesses. The random search for a factor is fast: we use the coin repeatedly to 'guess' digit after digit of the candidate, and then check whether the resulting number is indeed a good witness by carrying out a simple division. If we find that K divides the candidate evenly, we have conclusive evidence that K is composite, exactly as needed. The problem, however, is what to do if the division leaves a remainder. There are exponentially many numbers between 2 and $K - 1$ (that is, exponential in N, the length of K), and even if we manage to avoid checking multiples, there are still exponentially many candidates that might have to be checked if we want to stop trying at some point and declare K to be prime with only a very small chance of being wrong.

Put in simple words, there are too many potential places to look for a witness, and the actual witnesses are distributed too sparsely, so that trying to find one at random is like looking for a needle in a very large haystack.

To be able to utilize the witness idea, we must come up with different kinds of witnesses for non-primality. Just like factors, the new witnesses must also provide undisputable evidence of K's compositeness, but they must be distributed a lot more densely, so that a random probe is far more likely to find one — if there is one. Such witness definitions have indeed been discovered, and they are at the heart of the fast primality testing algorithms. We shall not get into the details of these witnesses here, but we should say a few words about their effect.

In one of these probabilistic primality testing algorithms, things are set up in such a way that if the input number K is composite, more than *half* of the numbers between 1 and $K–1$ are witnesses. This means that if you pick a number in this range at random, and it turns out *not* to be a witness to K's compositeness, you can be more than 50% certain that K is prime, since the probability of missing a witness when K is not prime is less than $\frac{1}{2}$. If you carry out the same thing again, choosing some other potential witness at random, and you don't hit upon a witness this time either, you can be 75% sure that K is prime. This is because the two random probes were carried out independently, so that the probabilities are multiplied, resulting in the probability of a miss becoming $\frac{1}{4}$. For three probes, the chance of missing a witness when K is composite is $\frac{1}{8}$, and our confidence in K's primality goes up to 87.5%, and so on. Thus, if we carry out R probes, the chance of missing a witness is 1 in 2^R.[9]

This translates immediately into an extremely fast probability testing algorithm. (See Fig. 5.2 for a schematic description.) Choose, say, 200 random numbers between 1 and $K–1$ and test each for being a witness to K's compositeness; stop and say 'No, K is not prime' if and when any one of them is found to be a witness, and stop and say 'Yes, K is prime' if they all pass the witness-testing

---

[9] We should add that checking whether a candidate number is a true witness can be done very efficiently, but since we have not provided the technical definition of a witness, we shall say no more on this matter here.

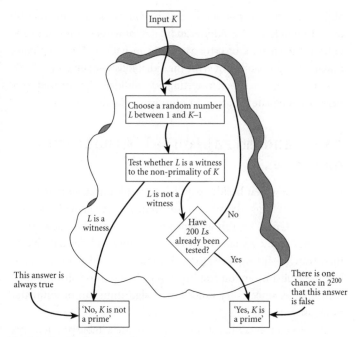

Fig. 5.2. Randomized primality testing.

procedure in the negative. We can always believe a 'No' coming from this algorithm, since finding a valid witness provides unshakable evidence that K is composite. When it outputs a 'Yes' we can believe it too, since although the algorithm *might* be wrong the chances are less than 1 in 2^{200}, which is unimaginably minute.

Recalling the Russian roulette story here, we conclude that this performance is more than adequate for any practical purpose. It can — and should! — be used freely even for cases where people's money or lives are at stake. Moreover, if such an incredible probability of success is not good enough, you can simply instruct the algorithm to test 201 random candidates for witness, instead of 200, cutting the chances of error yet again in half, or 500 candidates: making the probability of error the ridiculously small: 1 in 2^{500}. We might add that, in practice, testing 50 candidates has proved to be perfectly adequate for an input number of 200 digits or so.

can randomization eliminate the bad news?

We now know that besides parallelism randomization is also capable of providing dramatic improvements in algorithmic performance. Great. So, can we *now* forget about this bad news stuff?

No, not really. As far as raw computability and decidability go, the Church – Turing thesis extends to randomized algorithms too: like parallelism, randomization cannot be used to solve the non-computable, since every randomized algorithm can be simulated by a conventional one.

How about tractability? Can we turn an intractable problem into a tractable one using randomization? As in the case of parallelism, no-one knows. Some problems that are not known to be in PTIME, like primality testing, can be solved very fast using randomization, but we don't know if this can be done for a *provably* intractable problem. In fact, some problems that are conjectured to be intractable in the usual sense are conjectured to remain so even in the face of randomization. Factoring numbers is one example. Most researchers believe that the factoring problem, which asks for the factors of a composite number, is not solvable in polynomial time, even with coin-tossing (although we shall soon see that in the quantum world this is no longer true). We should add that allowing both parallelism *and* randomization doesn't make things significantly better, so that even in the presence of both kinds of liberty discussed so far, the bad news of the previous chapters remains standing, tall and firm.[10]

can computers simulate true randomness?

An issue that we should address is the way computers can be made to toss fair, unbiased coins. The problem is that a real digital computer is a totally deterministic entity; all of its actions can be

---

[10] The class RP stands for **random-PTIME**, problems solvable in polynomial time using Monte Carlo-type coin tossing algorithms for the 'Yes' direction. More precisely, RP contains the decision problems for which there is a polynomial-time coin tossing Turing machine with the following property. If the correct answer for an input X is 'No', the machine says 'No' with probability 1, and if the correct answer is 'Yes', it says 'Yes' with probability greater than $\frac{1}{2}$. Of course, the interest in RP stems from the fact that these possibly erroneous computations can be reiterated many times, achieving an exponentially diminishing probability of error, as explained for the fast primality testing algorithm. RP lies between PTIME and NP. Here too, many researchers believe that the inclusions are strict. Spelled out in words, these beliefs read as follows: (i) There are problems that can be solved in good time with magical nondeterminism that cannot be solved in good time without it even using randomization. (ii) There are problems that can be solved in good time with randomization that cannot be solved in good time without it. Adding RP to the symbolic summary given in an earlier footnote, we get:

$$\text{NC} \overset{?}{\subset} \text{PTIME} \overset{?}{\subset} \text{RP} \overset{?}{\subset} \text{NP} \overset{?}{\subset} \text{PSPACE} \; (= \text{parallel-PTIME})$$

It is thus interesting that in the realm of polynomial time we don't know whether coin tossing provides any real additional power, or whether magical coin tossing provides even more.

predicted in advance — at least in principle. Consequently, computers can't generate truly random numbers, and hence they can't simulate the truly random tossing of fair coins. So what can we do?

We could perhaps appeal to a physical source. For example, our computer could be attached to a small robot hand that scoops up some sand from a large container, counts the sand grains in the scoop, and decides 'Heads' if the number is even and 'Tails' otherwise. This approach has several obvious drawbacks. A more practical idea involves **pseudo-random numbers**. A pseudo-random sequence of '0's and '1's is one that cannot be distinguished from a truly random sequence in polynomial time. So, it's not *really* random but you'll never be able to tell the difference. This is perfectly satisfactory for our purposes, which will always involve solving problems in polynomial time: if no process can tell the difference between our computer's tosses and real random tosses in an acceptable amount of time, we are in good shape.

Unfortunately, however, no-one knows if pseudo-random numbers can themselves be generated in polynomial time! Computers that run randomized algorithms indeed have access to random number generators, and these appear to be satisfactory in practice. But whether the sequences they produce are actually pseudo-random (that is, whether they are really indistinguishable from true random ones in polynomial time) depends on open problems of the kind discussed earlier. Thus, rather curiously, not only do we not know whether randomized algorithms can turn intractable problems into tractable ones, but the very ability to generate the random numbers that are needed in such algorithms hinges on unknowns about the very nature of intractability. Yes, that does sound a little strange, but it's true nevertheless.

quantum computing

So what's all this fashionable new quantum computing stuff? Well, it is a deep and complicated topic, and one that is very hard to describe in the expository fashion of this book. It hinges upon quantum mechanics, a remarkable topic in modern physics, which is unfortunately slippery and difficult to grasp, and is often counter-intuitive. A lot of mathematics is needed to explain what is going on, since trying to employ worldly common sense to the quantum world can easily become a hindrance to comprehension rather than an aid. The following sections will thus read more like high-level ramblings than like a careful attempt at responsible exposition. My apologies for that (and several pointers to surveys in the literature for the more curious, mathematically adept reader[11]).

On the brighter side, there is a chance — a very small one as of the time of writing — that quantum computing could bring with it good news of the kind alluded to in this book. How, why, and when, are the questions we shall try to address, very briefly, and very superficially.

One of the main advantages of quantum physics is its ability to make sense out of certain experimental phenomena on the particle level, which classical physics seemed unable to do. Two of the main curiosities of the quantum world, stated very informally, are

---

[11] C. P. Williams and S. H. Clearwater (1998). *Explorations in Quantum Computing*. Springer-Verlag, New York; D. Aharonov (1998). 'Quantum Computation', *Annual Reviews of Computational Physics VI*; A. Berthiaume (1997). 'Quantum Computation', in *Complexity Theory Retrospective II* (Hemaspaandra and Selman, eds). Springer-Verlag, New York, pp. 23–51; M. Hirvensalo (1998). 'An introduction to quantum computation', *Bull. Europ. Assoc. for Theor. Comp. Sci.* **66**, October, 100–21.

that a particle can no longer be considered to be at a single location in space at a particular time, and that its situation (including location) can change as a result of merely observing it. The first of these seems like good news for computing: might we not be able to exploit the property of being at many places simultaneously to carry out massive parallelization of a computation? The second, however, seems like bad news: trying to 'see' or 'touch' a value during a computation, say, to carry out a comparison or an update, could change that value unpredictably!

Quantum computation has its roots in early work by Bennett and Benioff, but is considered to have first been proposed in 1982 by Richard Feynman, followed by a more detailed proposal by David Deutsch.[12] The motivating idea was that if a computer could be built that operates according to the laws of quantum physics, rather than those of classical physics, one might be able to obtain an exponential speedup for certain computations.

A quantum computer, like a classical one, is to be based on some kind of finite-state element, analogous to the classical 2-state bit. The quantum analog of a bit, called a **qubit**, can be envisioned physically in a number of ways: by the direction of photon polarization (horizontal or vertical), by nuclear spin (a special 2-valued quantum observable), or by the energy level of an atom (ground

---

[12] C. Bennett (1973). 'Logical Reversibility of Computation', *IBM J. Research and Development* **17**, 525–32; P. Benioff (1980). 'The Computer as a Physical System: A Microscopic Quantum Mechanical Hamiltonian Model of Computers as Represented by Turing Machines', *J. Stat. Phys.* **22**, 563–91; R. Feynman (1982). 'Quantum Mechanical Computers', *Optics News* **11**, 11–20; D. Deutsch (1985). 'Quantum Theory, the Church–Turing Principle, and the Universal Quantum Computer', *Proc. R. Soc. London* **A400**, 97–117.

or excited). The two so-called **basis states** of a qubit, analogous to the 0 and 1 of an ordinary bit, are denoted by $|0\rangle$ and $|1\rangle$, respectively. What we *don't* have in a quantum system is the simple deterministic notion of the qubit being in one basis state or another. Rather, its notion of being or not being is indeterminate: all we can say about the status of a qubit is that it is in both of the states simultaneously, each with a certain 'probability'. (Should we call this '*To qubee or not to qubee*'?) But, as if to deliberately make things even less comprehensible to mortals, these are not ordinary, positive-valued probabilities, like being in state $|0\rangle$ with probability $\frac{1}{4}$ and in $|1\rangle$ with probability $\frac{3}{4}$. The 'probabilities' can be negative, even imaginary (i.e. complex numbers that involve square roots of negatives), and the resulting combination state is called a **superposition**. Once we 'take a look' at a qubit, i.e. make a measurement, it suddenly decides where to be, we see it in one basis state or the other, the probabilities disappear and the superposition is forgotten.[13] This kind of 'forced discreteness' is what leads to the adjective 'quantum'.

So much for a single qubit. What happens with many qubits taken together, side by side, which we need as the basis for true quantum computation? How are the states of several qubits combined to obtain a compound state of the entire computing device? In the classical case, any collection of N bits, each of which can be in two states 0 or 1, gives rise to 2^N compound states. In the quantum world of qubits we also start with the 2^N compound states built from the

---

[13] Specifically, a superposition is what is sometimes called a complex unit-length linear combination of the basis states. That is, the coefficients are two complex numbers c_0 and c_1 satisfying $|c_0|^2 + |c_1|^2 = 1$. After measuring, we will 'see' a 0 with probability $|c_0|^2$ And a 1 with probability $|c_1|^2$.

basis states of N qubits (in the case of two qubits, for example, the four compound states are denoted $|00\rangle$, $|01\rangle$, $|10\rangle$ and $|11\rangle$). To these we then apply complex combinations, just as we did for a single qubit. However, here, the way the combinations are defined gives rise to an additional crucial twist called, appropriately, **entanglement**: some of the compound states are clean composites that can be obtained — using an operation called a 'tensor product' — from the states of the original qubits, but some can't; they are entangled. Entangled qubits, a term that comes with a precise mathematical rendition, represent an intrinsically non-separable 'mish-mash' of the original qubits. They have the weird property of instant communication: observing one and thus fixing its state causes the other to lock in the dual state simultaneously, no matter how far away they are from each other. Entanglement turns out to be a fundamental and indispensable notion in quantum computation, but unfortunately further discussion of its technicalities and the way it is exploited in the computations themselves is beyond the scope of this book.

quantum algorithms

What have people been able to do with quantum computation?

A few facts have to be stated up front. First, full, general-purpose quantum computing subsumes classical computation. That is, if and when built, a quantum computer will be able to emulate classical computations without any significant loss of time. Second, although seemingly weaker, a classical computer can still simulate any quantum computation, but this could entail an exponential loss of time. The fact that this simulation is possible means that quantum computation cannot destroy the Church–Turing thesis:

computability remains intact in the world of quantum computation too. If and when actual quantum computers are built, they will not be able to solve problems not solvable without them.

This having been said, the big question is whether the exponential loss of time in the second statement is indeed insurmountable. Exactly as we did with parallelism and randomization, we ask whether there are provably intractable problems that become tractable in the quantum world. That is, is there a problem with an exponential-time lower bound in the classical models of computation that has a polynomial-time quantum algorithm?[14]

Computation complexity aside, and the technological issue of actually building a quantum computer notwithstanding, there have already been some extremely exciting developments in quantum algorithmics. Here are some of the highlights.

Deutsch showed how to achieve quantum parallelism, whereby superposition of the inputs is used to produce a superposition of outputs.[15] Interestingly, although this seems as though one is indeed computing lots of stuff in parallel, the outputs cannot be naïvely separated out and read from their superposition; any attempt at reading, or measuring, will produce only one output

---

[14] And as we did in earlier footnotes, if we use QP to stand for **quantum-PTIME**, the open issues become:

$$\text{PTIME} \overset{?}{\subset} \text{RP} \overset{?}{\subset} \text{QP} \overset{?}{\subset} \text{PSPACE} \ (= \text{parallel-PTIME})$$

Thus, good quantum time lies around the same place as NP, i.e. between good random time and good memory space. Unfortunately, as before, we do not know whether any of the inclusions are strict.

[15] D. Deutsch (1985). 'Quantum Theory, the Church–Turing Principle, and the Universal Quantum Computer', *Proc. R. Soc. London* **A400**, 97–117.

and the rest will simply be lost. What is needed is for the algorithm to cleverly compute *joint* properties common to all outputs, and make do with them. Examples might include certain arithmetical aggregate values of numerical outputs, or the 'and's and 'or's of logical yes/no outputs.[16]

Later, Grover discovered a rather surprising quantum algorithm for searching in an unordered list, say a large database. Instead of using around N operations, an item can be found with $\sqrt{N}$ operations only (the square root of N). This is counter-intuitive, almost paradoxical, since it would appear necessary to at least *look* at all N inputs in order to figure out whether what you are searching for is indeed there.[17]

However, the big surprise, and indeed the pinnacle of quantum algorithms so far, is Peter Shor's factoring algorithm. We have mentioned factoring several times in the book, and its importance as a central algorithmic problem is undisputable. As we have seen, factoring has not yet been shown to be tractable in the usual sense — it is not known to be in PTIME, and the very fact that it appears to be computationally difficult plays a critical role in cryptography, as we shall see in Chapter 6. So much so, in fact, that a significant part of the walls that hold up modern cryptography would come

---

[16] However, there are results that show that this ability is inherently limited. While the use of quantum parallelism can often yield significant gains in efficiency, it is unable to deliver each and every desired joint property. See R. Josza (1991). 'Characterizing Classes of Functions Computable by Quantum Parallelism', *Proc. R. Soc. London* **A435**, 563-74.

[17] L. Grover (1996). 'A Fast Quantum Mechanical Algorithm for Database Search', *Proc. 28th Ann. ACM Symp. on Theory of Computing*, pp. 212–19. This technique enables similar quadratic speedups for all problems in NP.

tumbling down if an efficient factoring algorithm would become available. It is against this background that one should view the significance of Shor's work, which provides a polynomial-time quantum algorithm for the problem.[18]

To appreciate the subtlety of quantum factoring, consider a naïve algorithm that attempts to find the factors of a number N by trial and error, going through all pairs of potential factors and multiplying them to see if their product is exactly N. Why shouldn't we be able to do this using grand-scale quantum parallelism? We could use quantum variables to hold a superposition of all candidate factors (say, all numbers between 0 and $\sqrt{N}$), then compute, in parallel, and in the best quantum spirit, all products of all possible pairs of these numbers. We could then try to check whether there was a pair that did the job. Unfortunately, this wouldn't work, since taking a look at — that is, carrying out a measurement of — this enormous superposed output would not say much. We might just happen to hit upon a factorization, but we might also land on any other of the many products that are different from N. And as we have already mentioned, once you measure, that's what you get to see, and the rest is lost. So, just the mish-mashing of lots of information, that alone, is not enough.

It turns out that things have to be arranged so that there is **inter-ference**. This is a quantum notion, whereby the possible solutions 'fight' each other for supremacy in subtle ways. The ones that turn

---

[18] P. Shor (1994). 'Algorithms for Quantum Computation: Discrete Logarithms and Factoring', *Proc. 35th Ann. Symp. On Found. Comp. Sci.*, pp. 124–34; P. Shor (1997). *SIAM J. Comp.* **26**(5), 1484. Shor's work relies on D. Simon (1994). 'On the Power of Quantum Computation', *Proc. 35th Ann. IEEE Symp. On Found. Comp. Sci.*, pp. 116-23.

out not to be good solutions (in our case, pairs of numbers whose product is not N) will interfere *de*structively in the superposition, and the ones that are good solutions (their product is N) will interfere *con*structively. The results of this fight will then show up as varying amplitudes in the output, so that measuring the output superposition will give the good solutions a much better shot at showing up. We should remark that it is the negative numbers in the definition of superposition that make this kind of interference possible in a quantum algorithm.

This is easier said than done, and it is here that the mathematics of quantum computing gets complicated and is beyond the scope and level of our exposition. But what we can say is that the right kind of entanglement has been achieved for factoring. The algorithm itself is quite remarkable, both in its technique, and as we shall see later, in its ramifications.[19]

This algorithm hasn't yet turned a provably intractable problem into a tractable one, for two reasons, one of which we have repeatedly mentioned and one of which we have hinted at but will shortly address in more detail. First, factoring isn't *known* to be intractable; we simply haven't been able to find a polynomial-time algorithm for it. It is *conjectured* to be hard, but we are not sure. Second, no-one yet knows how to build a quantum computer capable of implementing Shor's algorithm.

---

[19] Its time performance is roughly cubic, that is, not much more than M^3, where M is the number of digits in the input number N. For the more technically interested reader, what Shor actually did was to find an efficient quantum method to compute the order of a number Y modulo N, that is, to find the least integer a such that $Y^a = 1 \pmod{N}$. This is known to be enough to enable fast factoring, and the rest of the work is done using conventional algorithms.

can there be a quantum computer?

When discussing parallelism earlier, we noted that there is a certain mismatch between existing parallel algorithms and the parallel computers that have been built to run them. To be efficiently implemented, many known algorithms require hardware features not yet available, and, dually, the theory of parallel algorithms has yet to catch up with what the available hardware *is* able to do.

In the realm of quantum computation the situation is less symmetric. We have at our disposal some really nice quantum algorithms, but no machines whatsoever to run them on.

Why? Again, the issue revolves around deep technicalities, but this time the barrier preventing a detailed exposition here is not the mathematics but the physics. So, again, we shall only provide a very brief account, and the interested reader will have to seek more information elsewhere.[20]

At the time of writing (actually, the proof-reading; early-2000), the largest quantum 'computer' that has actually been built consists of a mere seven qubits. This is not a typing error; *seven qubits.* What is the problem? Why can't we scale up?

Despite the fact that the quantum algorithms themselves, and Shor's in particular, are designed to work according to rigorous and widely accepted principles of quantum physics, there are severe technical problems around the actual building of a

---

[20] D. P DiVincenzo (1995). 'Quantum Computation', *Science* **270**, 255–61; A. Berthiaume (1997). 'Quantum Computation', in *Complexity Theory Retrospective II* (Hemaspaandra and Selman, eds.). Springer-Verlag, New York, pp. 23–51; C. P. Williams and S. H. Clearwater (1998). *Explorations in Quantum Computing.* Springer-Verlag, New York.

quantum computer. First, experimental physicists have not managed to be able to put even a small number of qubits (say, 20) together and control them in some reasonable way. The difficulties seem beyond present-day laboratory techniques. A particularly troubling issue is **decoherence**: even if you could gather a good number of qubits and cause them to behave nicely themselves, things that reside close to a quantum system have the pushy habit of affecting it. The quantum behavior of anything surrounding a quantum computer — the casing, the walls, the people, the keyboard, *anything*! — can mess up the delicate setup of constructive and destructive interference within the quantum computation. Even a single naughty electron can affect the interference pattern that is so crucial for the correct execution of the algorithm, by becoming entangled with the qubits participating in that execution, and as a result the desired superposition could fail.

The computer thus has to be relentlessly isolated from its environment. But it also has to read inputs and produce an output, and its computational process might have to be controlled by some external elements. Somehow, these contradictory requirements have to be reconciled.

What kind of sizes do we really need? Some small-scale quantum coding protocols require only something like 15–20 qubits, and even Shor's algorithm needs only a few thousand qubits to be applicable in real-world situations. But since experimental physics can barely deal with six or seven qubits right now, and even that is *extremely* difficult, many people are pessimistic. A true breakthrough is not expected any time soon. On the brighter side, the excitement surrounding the topic is already bringing about a flurry of ideas and proposals, accompanied by complex laboratory experimentation, so that we are bound to see interesting advances in the near future.

In summary, Shor's factoring algorithm constitutes a major advance by any measure. However, at the moment it must be relegated to the status of shelfware, and it is probably destined to remain that way for quite some time.

Intractability hasn't been beaten yet.

molecular computing

To wrap up our discussion of models of computation aimed at trying to alleviate some of the bad news, we mention one more: **molecular computing**, sometimes called **DNA computing**.

The main approach here, which was first exhibited in 1994 by Len Adleman[21], is based on letting the computation happen essentially on its own, in a carefully concocted 'soup' of molecules, that play with each other, splitting, joining and merging. Thus, you get billions or trillions of molecules to tackle a hard problem by brute force, setting things up cleverly so that the winning cases can later be isolated and identified.

In the experiment Adleman actually carried out he got molecules to solve a small instance of the Hamiltonian path problem, which is a sort of unit-length version of the traveling salesman problem. Later, other problems — essentially all problems in NP — were shown to be amenable to similar techniques.[22]

---

[21] L. M. Adelman (1994). 'Molecular Computation of Solutions to Combinatorial Problems', *Science* **266**, 1021–4.

[22] R. J. Lipton (1994). 'DNA Solution of Hard Computational Problems', *Science* **268**, 542–5; L. M. Adelman (1998). 'Computing with DNA', *Scientific American* **279** (2), 34–41. A recent book on the topic is G. Paun, G. Rozenberg, and A. Salomaa (1998). *DNA Computing.*

continued on next page

That nature can be tuned to solve real-world algorithmic problems, essentially all by itself, and on a molecular scale, is rather astonishing. While Adleman's original experiment, for a seven-city instance, took about a week in the laboratory, the problem was solved later by others in less of a brute-force fashion, and for much larger instances (50–60 cities). Dedicating molecular biology labs to this kind of work can result in a significant speeding up of the process, and indeed lots of work is under way to try to get the techniques to scale up.

From a puristic point of view, things are reminiscent of conventional parallel algorithms: although in principle the time complexity of such molecular algorithms is polynomial because of the high degree of parallelism that goes on within the molecular soup, the number of molecules involved in the process grows exponentially. But on the positive side, one of the main advantages of using DNA is its incredible information density. Some results show that DNA computations may use a billion times less energy than an electronic computer doing the same things, and could store data in a trillion times less space.[23]

In any case, molecular computing is definitely another exciting area of research, catching the imagination and energy of many talented computer scientists and biologists. We are bound to see a

continued
Springer-Verlag, Berlin. Surveys are S. A. Kurtz, S. R. Mahaney, J. S. Royer, and J. Simon (1997). 'Biological Computing', in *Complexity Theory Retrospective II*, (Hemanspaandra and Selman eds.). Springer-Verlag, New York, pp. 179–95; L. Kari (1997). 'DNA computing: The arrival of biological mathematics', *The Mathematical Intelligencer* **19** (2), 9–22.

[23] E. Baum (1995). 'Building an associative memory vastly larger than the brain', *Science* **268** (April), 583–5.

lot of exciting work in this area in the future, and some specific difficult problems might very well become doable for reasonably sized inputs. Still, we must remember that molecular computing can definitely not eliminate noncomputability, nor is it expected to do away with the woeful effects of intractability.

This brings our account of the bad news in algorithmics to an end. Ignoring the slim rays of hope offered by quantum and molecular computing, a brief summary of Chapters 2–5 might go like this:

> What we know about for sure is bad enough already.
>
> Figuring out the answers to the questions that remain open
> might make things a little better
> but will probably make them a lot worse.
>
> And what's really frustrating
> is the uncertainty that comes from not really knowing.

chapter 6
turning bad into good

This chapter is devoted to cryptography, one of the most interesting application areas of algorithmics and a wonderful source of research challenges.

Increasingly, computers are used for storing, manipulating, generating, and transmitting data. This includes critical and delicate information, such as commercial contracts, military and intelligence reports, business transactions, and personal items of confidential nature such as credit card numbers and medical or financial data. This situation, in turn, makes problems of eavesdropping, theft, and forgery all the more acute, resulting in the need for extensive cryptographic mechanisms for the secure and reliable communication of information.

Modern day cryptography is of particular relevance to this book because of its most unusual and striking feature: subtle and unabashed exploitation of the bad news in computing. This is surprising. In fact, it sounds impossible, and appears to have very few counterparts in other branches of human endeavor. How can you use one thing's impossibility to make another thing possible that was otherwise impossible too? If we pause to think about it, we would expect nothing of any value to come of negative results in algorithmics, except in helping prevent people from wasting time trying to do things that can't be done. Nevertheless, problems for which we have no good solutions are crucial here; in fact, if they turn out to have good solutions we are in big trouble!

No news is good news, the saying goes. This chapter will show that *bad* news can sometimes be good news too.

classical cryptography

The basic activities in cryptography are encoding and decoding, often called encryption and decryption. We want to be able to encode a message in such a way that the recipient should be able to decode it, but an eavesdropper shouldn't. As an example, a general might want to order a subordinate colonel to attack at dawn, without the enemy being able to intercept and decipher the message.

But there is more to this scenario than just secrecy and defending against eavesdropping. If the attack is undertaken and it fails, the colonel might want to blame the general for having given a bad order; or the general might want to shake off responsibility by claiming that he didn't send the message (he could claim that the enemy did it to lure them into an ambush, or that the colonel forged the message for some reason). This leads to the need to allow the sender to 'sign' messages. In this way, (i) the recipient can be sure that the sender alone could have sent it, (ii) the sender cannot later deny having sent it, and (iii) the recipient, having received the signed message, cannot forge the signature and sign another message in the sender's name, not even a copy of the original message. The signature issue adds another level of difficulty to the basic encryption issue, but it is central to many applications of cryptography, such as military communications, money transfer orders, and signing contracts.

Conventional cryptosystems are based on **keys**, which are used to translate a message M — sometimes called the **plaintext** — into its encrypted form M^* — sometimes called the **ciphertext** — and then to decrypt M^* back into its original form. If we denote the general encryption procedure associated with the key by encode, and the corresponding decryption procedure by decode, we may write:

$$M^* = \mathsf{encode}(M) \quad \text{and} \quad M = \mathsf{decode}(M^*)$$

In words, the encrypted version M^* is obtained by applying the encode procedure to the message M. The original M in turn can be retrieved from M^* by applying the decode procedure to it.

What do keys look like? A simple example that we have all used in our childhood calls for the key to be a number K between 1 and 25, chosen and shared by both parties, the sender (encoder) and the receiver (decoder). The encode procedure replaces every letter with the one residing K positions further along in the alphabet, and decode replaces every letter with the one residing K positions earlier. In this way, encode and decode are mutually dual: you use decode to undo what encode did, and vice versa. For the purpose of counting letters, the alphabet is considered to be cyclic, so that *a* follows *z*. For example, if K is 6, '*My Fair Lady*' becomes '*Se Lgox Rgje*'. Pretty indeed ....

This simple approach can be illustrated using the metaphor of a locked box. To set up a method to exchange secret messages with a friend, you first prepare a box with a securable latch. The two of you then go out and buy a padlock with two identical keys, one for you and one for your friend. Thereafter, sending a message involves putting it in the box, locking the box using the key, and sending the box to its destination. No-one without access to the key can read the message *en route*. Since there are only two keys, kept by the sender and the intended recipient, the system is secure.

This approach has several drawbacks. First, it requires that the two parties cooperate in the selection and safe distribution of keys. Either they must both go out together to buy the lock and keys, or the one who buys them must later find a way to transfer one of the keys safely and securely to the other. If we leave the locked box metaphor for a moment, returning to computerized communication, this means that setting up a secure channel requires first sending something over a secure channel, which is rather ridiculous. We can't use the usual computerized network for distributing keys because the cryptographic framework hasn't been set up yet and an eavesdropper would be able to get hold of them and ruin the whole thing. Moreover, real applications involve many parties, often located at great distances — just think of people wanting to send each other credit card numbers over the Internet. To enable private communication between any two of the parties we have to distribute different keys to each different pair. Using specialized secure methods for this, such as personal delivery by a trusted courier, is simply out of the question.

The other major drawback of naïve cryptographic methods is that they don't address the signature issue at all. If it's not just friendly communication that is taking place, but, say, secret trading negotiations between competing companies, all kinds of nasty things can happen. The recipient can make up fake messages and claim they were sent by the sender; the sender can deny having sent authentic messages, and so on. The ability to sign a message is thus very important.

public-key cryptography

In 1976, Diffie and Hellman proposed a novel approach to the encryption, decryption, and signature problems, called **public-key cryptography**.[1] It can also be explained by the locked box metaphor. The idea is to use a different kind of padlock: a key is required to *un*lock it, but it can be locked by a simple click, without a key. To set up the communication system, each of the two participants goes out all alone and purchases a personal click-close padlock and key. Each of them then writes his or her name on the padlock, and places it on the table, in public view. The key is not disclosed or shown to anyone else at all. Now, assume party *B* — say, Bob — wants to send a message to party *A* — say, Alice. Bob puts the message into a box, goes to the public table, picks up Alice's padlock and locks the box with it. This he does simply by clicking her padlock shut; he doesn't need her key. The box is then sent to Alice, who uses her key to open the lock and read the message. Since no-one has had access to her key except for Alice herself, the message is safe. Remarkably, no prior communication or cooperation between Alice and Bob is needed. Moreover, this scheme is not limited to two participants. The public table can host as many padlocks as there are parties who want to participate in mutual communication. As long as each participant has his or her own padlock and keeps the key safe, they are all in business!

---

[1] W. Diffie and M. Hellman (1976). 'New Directions in Cryptography', *IEEE Trans. Inform. Theory* **IT-22**, 644-54.

To understand how public-key systems can be used in digital, computerized environments, we assume that messages are (perhaps lengthy) sequences of digits. Thus, some direct and straightforward method of translating letters and symbols into digits has already been applied. Alice's padlock is really just an encryption function encode that transforms numbers into other numbers, and her key embodies a secret way of computing the decryption function decode. Thus, each party makes its encryption procedure public but keeps its decryption procedure private. For the most part, we shall stick to two participants — our friends Alice and Bob. To distinguish between the different functions they use, we shall denote Alice's by $encode_A$ and $decode_A$, and Bob's by $encode_B$ and $decode_B$.

In order to send the number M as a message to Alice, Bob uses Alice's public encryption procedure $encode_A$ and sends her the ciphertext $encode_A(M)$, which is the number obtained by applying the function $encode_A$ to the number M. Again, it is *Alice's* function that Bob uses, just as in the padlock analogy. Alice would then decipher this number using her private decryption procedure $decode_A$, yielding the original message M (i.e. the plaintext). This is illustrated in Fig. 6.1. As a simple example (which can't really be used, as we shall see, but is nevertheless illustrative) Alice might have chosen her encryption procedure $encode_A$ to be the function that squares its argument, and $decode_A$ to be the function that extracts square roots. Thus Bob would send her the number M^2 as the ciphertext and she would compute $\sqrt{M^2}$ to obtain the original plaintext M.

For the method to work, both functions must be easy to compute, and the two must be perfect inverses of each other, just as with squaring and extracting roots. Specifically, the following

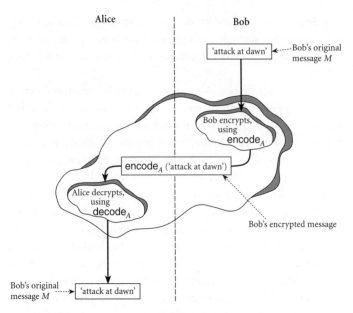

Fig. 6.1. Public-key encryption and decryption.

equation must be true for every possible message M, meaning that encoding M and decoding the encoding (both done using Alice's functions) must result in the original M.

$$\mathsf{decode}_A(\mathsf{encode}_A(M)) = M$$

But that's not all. It must be *impossible* to deduce a method for figuring out the decryption function decode_A from the publicly known encryption function encode_A. We want Alice to be able to decrypt easily, but for no-one else to be able to do so, even by closely inspecting the publicly known encryption function. This requirement is clearly violated by the squaring and root-taking functions, since once you know that encryption involves squaring, you know that decryption involves extracting the square root, which would be as easy for anyone to carry out as it is for Alice herself.

What we really need is a **one-way trapdoor function**, and here is where the keys enter the game. We want the encryption function encode$_A$ to be computable easily, but not the decryption function decode$_A$. This we take to mean that *the former should be in poly-nomial time and the latter shouldn't*, unless Alice's secret key is known. The key is what Alice needs in order to decode efficiently (again, just like in the padlock metaphor). The same should apply to Bob's functions encode$_B$ and decode$_B$; that is, encode$_B$ should be computable in acceptable time, but not decode$_B$ except for Bob, who has his key. The term 'one-way' is used to hint at the easiness of computing one direction — encoding — vs. the difficulty of computing the other — decoding — without a key. The analogy to trapdoors is this: a trapdoor cannot be activated unless you know the location of the secret lever (the key).

It is by no means clear how to find such functions. We can try to elaborate on the squaring and root-taking idea, with Alice setting up her encryption function to raise the plaintext to some higher power, for example, to compute M^7. This will make the extraction of the 7th root somewhat harder, but neither of the two crucial require-ments is met: first, once you know that encryption involves raising the plaintext to the 7th power, you know what to do for decryption, and second, decryption is still no harder for you than it is for Alice. The mathematical setup will have to be more sophisticated, and must involve a secret piece of information — the key — that makes decryption easy (for Alice), but whose absence renders it very, very hard (e.g. for Bob). We shall discuss this issue a little later.

signing messages

What makes a signature a signature? It goes without saying that a signature must be specialized for the person doing the signing: to prevent forgery the signatures of any two people must be sufficiently different. But a conventional handwritten signature doesn't have to depend on the *document*. In fact, a handwritten signature should look the same whenever and wherever it is used. In contrast, **digital signatures** of the kind we would like to use in a computerized cryptosystem, must be different not only for any two signers but also for any two messages being signed. Otherwise, when in dispute, a recipient could make changes to a signed message before showing it to a neutral judge, or could even attach the signature to a completely different message. If the message is a money-transfer order, the recipient could simply add a couple of carefully-placed zeros to the sum and claim the new signed message to be authentic. Our signatures must thus depend on both the signer and the message being signed.

A remarkable fact about the public-key cryptographic framework is that it can be used for signatures too. All we need is that the one-way trapdoor functions used for encryption and decryption be *mutual* inverses. This means that not only should the decryption of any encrypted message yield the original plaintext, but the *en*cryption of a *de*crypted message should also yield the original message. With squaring and root-extracting not only does $\sqrt{M^2}$ — taking the root of a square — yield the original M, but so does $(\sqrt{M})^2$ — squaring the root. Thus, for Alice's functions we require not only that

$$\mathsf{decode}_A(\mathsf{encode}_A(M)) = M$$

but also that

$$\mathsf{encode}_A(\mathsf{decode}_A(M)) = M$$

And the same for Bob's.

Why on earth would anyone be interested in decrypting a message that wasn't even encrypted? The answer: in order to sign it. Here is how it works (see Fig. 6.2).[2] If Bob wants to send Alice a signed message, he first applies his own private decryption function decode_B to the message M. This yields a number S, which we shall regard as Bob's special message-dependent signature:

$$S = \mathsf{decode}_B(M)$$

Then, instead of encrypting the original plaintext M for Alice, Bob encrypts the signed version thereof, S. This he does in the usual public-key fashion, using Alice's public encryption function encode_A. He then sends her the result, namely $\mathsf{encode}_A(S)$, which is really $\mathsf{encode}_A(\mathsf{decode}_B(M))$.

Cut now to Alice. Upon receiving this strange-looking number, Alice first decrypts it using her private decryption function decode_A. The result is $\mathsf{decode}_A(\mathsf{encode}_A(S))$. However, since decode_A undoes anything encode_A has 'messed up', i.e. the decode_A and the encode_A cancel each other out, the result of this will be S, which is really just $\mathsf{decode}_B(M)$. At this point, Alice can't read the message M yet, nor can she be sure that Bob was really the sender. But what she does now is to apply Bob's public encryption function encode_B to S. This yields M, because

$$\mathsf{encode}_B(S) = \mathsf{encode}_B(\mathsf{decode}_B(M)) = M$$

---

[2] The locked-box metaphor is inappropriate for explaining how public-key signatures work, as it makes little sense to unlock a box that wasn't even closed.

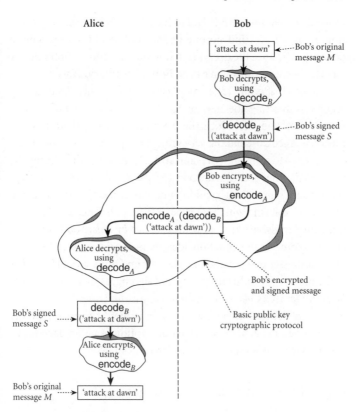

Fig. 6.2. Encryption with signatures.

Thus, all at once, Alice gets to see the original message M and can also be quite sure that only Bob could have sent it. How is this? Well, since the functions we use are carefully selected mutual inverses, no number except $decode_B(M)$ will result in M when subjected to $encode_B$. So it couldn't be anything else that happened to yield the plaintext M; it *had* to have been Bob's decoding function applied to M. But no-one besides Bob could have produced $\mathsf{decode}_B(M)$, since the decryption function decode_B is Bob's closely guarded secret! It must have been Bob. Elementary, Watson…

Alice can't sign any other message in Bob's name, since signing requires subjecting the new or modified message to Bob's secret function decode_B, to which she has no access. But there is still a problem. Alice can send the very same message M — but with Bob's signature — to someone else, say Carol. The reason is that during the process Alice has access to $\mathsf{decode}_B(M)$, which she can then encrypt using Carol's public encryption function encode_C, and send the result to Carol, who will think it came from Bob. This could be critical with a message like '*I, General Bob, hereby order you to attack at dawn*'. To prevent this situation, identifying details, such as the name of the addressee and possibly also the date and time, should be added to the message prior to encrypting and signing, as in '*I, General Bob, hereby order you, Colonel Alice, on this day … and time … to attack at dawn*'. Now Alice has no way to do mischief at Carol's expense, because she can't apply Bob's secret decryption function decode_B to any message that is even slightly different from M.

can this be made to work?

All this sounds very promising. A group of participants can communicate safely, guarded against eavesdroppers and other evils. They can send, receive, sign, verify, identify, etc. But how do we actually do it? What is the math needed? We have to figure out a method of defining the keys for each participant and the corresponding encode and decode procedures, but in such a way that all the nice properties we have discussed will hold true. Encoding must be easy, and decoding not, unless you have the key, and encoding and decoding must be perfect mutual inverses. Also, we have to be able to generate lots of different pairs of such functions, one for each participant (just as there are many different padlocks in a hardware store — with different keys).

At first glance, the requirements appear to be paradoxical. Where do we find a function that is easy to compute but has a really hard-to-compute inverse that becomes easy only when some secret key is available? As we saw earlier, squaring vs. extracting roots fails miserably, as do simple K-step shifts in the alphabet.

So, are there any such one-way trapdoor functions?

From a puristic point of view, the answer is that we don't know. However, in an important pragmatic sense the answer is a resounding yes, and public-key cryptography — signatures and all — is very much alive, well, kicking and working. First, though, we should elaborate on what it means for a public-key cryptosystem to be broken, or cracked. The integrity of the whole setup hinges on the fact that without access to the private key it is very difficult to apply a participant's **decode** function to a given number. To use the terminology of the last two chapters, very hard is intractable: we want **decode**, as an algorithmic problem, to be tractable if the key is given, but to be intractable without it. It should be computable in polynomial time *with* the key, but not computable in polynomial time without it. In contrast, the **encode** function should be tractable as it is; no key is needed. This means that to break the system you have to find a polynomial-time algorithm for computing the **decode** function without the key; that is, to show that the desired intractability fails.

Thus, cracking a public-key cryptosystem doesn't involve sly detective work or clever guessing. It is not even a matter of brute-force number-crunching on a large and fast computer. It is not

World War II-style battles of the brains, with cryptographic teams alternately outsmarting each other. Rather, it entails coming up with a polynomial-time algorithm for a problem that is believed to be of inherent super-polynomial-time behavior. And this is algorithmic work *par excellence.*

The best thing would be to base public-key cryptography on a *provably* intractable decode function. For example, if the hard direction of the one-way trapdoor function could be based in some way on the roadblock problem of Chapter 3, the system would be provably unbreakable, and therefore as secure as could be. As it stands, this has not yet been achieved. The only one-way trapdoor functions that have been discovered to date are based on decode functions whose intractability is *conjectured*, not actually known. They are believed to be secure, but we don't know for sure. The conjectured-to-be-intractable problems lying at the heart of most public-key cryptosystems are well known, and have withstood long and extensive attempts by many mathematicians and computer scientists at finding polynomial-time algorithms. We can thus be pretty confident of their intractability. That a person or agency interested in breaking a cryptosystem would have been able to solve some celebrated and long-standing open problem in the deep mathematics of intractability is unlikely.

the RSA cryptosystem

The first successful implementation of public-key cryptography has become known as the **RSA method.**[3] While a number of other

---

[3] RSA stands for the initials of its inventors; see R. L. Rivest, A. Shamir, and L. Adleman (1978). 'A Method for Obtaining Digital Signatures and Public-Key Cryptosystems', *Comm. Assoc. Comput. Mach.* **21**, 120–6.

methods exist, the RSA approach is probably the most interesting of them all. It is now over 20 years old, and, as we shall see, there's good reason to believe that it is really unbreakable.

The RSA method is based on the contrast between testing a number for primality and finding its factors. The heart of the method is the choice of keys and padlocks. Each participant, say Alice, secretly and at random, chooses two large prime numbers P and Q, of length, say, around 200 digits, and multiplies them, resulting in the product $P \times Q$, which would have around 400 digits.

Alice keeps her two primes secret, but makes their product public. It suffices to say that, given the product, no-one can find the two prime factors in an acceptable amount of time. As discussed in Chapter 5, there are no known fast methods, not even probabilistic ones, for factoring very large numbers, and Shor's polynomial-time quantum algorithm will not become implementable in the forseeable future.

Alice's encryption function encode$_A$ is constructed from the product $P \times Q$. Her decryption function decode$_A$ requires the product too, but also the primes P and Q themselves. Thus, anyone can encrypt a message addressed to her using the publicly available number $P \times Q$, but decrypting is possible only by Alice herself, since she is the only person with access to P and Q. Anyone else wanting to get their hands on P and Q in order to decrypt a message would have to factor $P \times Q$. We shall not get into details of the method itself here, as it is technically involved, but we should discuss how Alice is able to choose the large primes to begin with.

The infinitely many prime numbers are spread out over the entire spectrum of positive integers in a rather dense way. For example, there are 168 primes less than 1000, and about 78 500 primes less than a million. Among all 100-digit numbers, roughly one in every 300 is prime, and for 200-digit numbers it is about one in every 600.[4] To generate a new large prime number of length, say, between 180 and 220 digits, Alice uses the fact that testing for primality can be carried out very fast, using the probabilistic algorithms discussed in Chapter 5. And what she actually does is this: she generates, at random, odd numbers in that range repeatedly (by tossing coins to choose the digits and to decide exactly how long the number should be), and tests each one for primality until she hits one that is prime. There is an extremely high likelihood that she will find one within the first 1500 attempts, and a pretty good chance that she will find one much earlier. In any event, if she is careful not to choose the same number twice, she is sure to find one very fast using even a small personal computer. The problem of generating large primes efficiently is therefore reduced to that of testing the primality of large numbers, which we know how to carry out efficiently.

We thus have a cryptographic method that exploits the crucial difference between testing numbers for primality and factoring them into their prime factors. It makes essential use of good news — clever probabilistic algorithms for finding primes — and relies in a crucial way on bad news too — the apparent intractability of factoring large numbers. If anyone ever manages to factor large numbers acceptably fast, the entire RSA system would immediately collapse, since an adversary could take the public product $P \times Q$, find its factors P and Q, and use them to decode Alice's messages. In particular, if the polynomial-time quantum algorithm for factoring

---

[4] More generally, the number of primes less than a given number K is of the order of $K/\log_2 K$.

ever becomes practical, i.e. if appropriate quantum computers somehow get built, the RSA method will probably become useless.

Still, people do rely on RSA, they know it is safe now and believe it will remain so. Another way of putting it is that the many users of the RSA method start their day praying that what we think is bad news regarding the factoring problem will indeed remain so.[5]

interactive proofs

Cryptography and cryptographic protocols are useful for much more than transmitting messages. Recent years have seen an

---

[5] Two points are in line here. First, the size of the numbers to be factored is very important, even without a general polynomial-time algorithm at our disposal. In early 1999, a 140-digit number was factored using several hundred computers running for several months. Soon afterwards an optical device called Twinkle was devised by A. Shamir (but at the time of writing this has not yet been actually built). With around a dozen Twinkles — assuming they can be built — we would be able to factor 160-digit numbers within a few days only. This would force many RSA users to enlarge their keys considerably, since most applications of RSA use 512-bit numbers, which are between 154 and 155 decimal digits long and fall easily within the 160-digit range. The second point involves the converse of the statement that if we can factor fast, RSA must collapse: does the collapse of RSA actually entail fast factoring, or is there perhaps another way of breaking the RSA? This is not known, as no-one in a large community of expert researchers has yet proposed an approach to breaking the RSA system that does not entail a fast solution to the factoring problem. However, there is a slightly different version of the RSA system, due to M. O. Rabin, whose breakability is *provably* equivalent to fast factoring. In other words, for this particular cryptosystem it has been proved mathematically that any possible method for cracking it will yield a fast factoring algorithm. It would be nice to be able to make this stronger statement about the original RSA system too. However, no-one has been able to prove it yet.

extraordinary surge in the development of sophisticated methods for carrying out all manner of computerized interaction in the presence of adversaries, with the latter not being limited to eavesdroppers only. The rapid proliferation of the Internet, and its use in increasingly varied application areas, is a rich source of new problems. These then give rise to new ideas and methods.

In many of these applications, **interaction** is a central feature. Here is an example. Suppose two parties want to toss a coin between them, but they are far away and don't trust each other. A realistic case could be a couple getting divorced. The husband and wife cannot, or will not, get together face to face — perhaps they live in different cities — but they want to divide their property. They might be at the point of deciding about the house vs. the Picasso in the living room, and for this they want to toss a coin. Being connected to each other via computers and modems (or their lawyers being so connected), it seems that this is not possible. Say they somehow agree on who's Heads and who's Tails, how do they actually toss the coin? If one does the tossing the other might not believe the reported result or the tosser might lie about the result. Possibly both. Can this be done electronically by two untrusting parties located remotely and connected by their home computers only? The answer is yes. There is a clever and very fast protocol for this. It requires the two computers to interact back and forth electronically, and rather extensively. Again, we do not provide the details of this protocol, but we should remark that it too is based on factoring: on the assumption that factoring is indeed intractable, the result of this interaction will be a totally impartial association of Heads with one of the parties and Tails with the other. The husband and wife can both be perfectly confident that no cheating of any kind was possible, and neither of them can later try to get out of the deal, since the results can be subjected to legal scrutiny.[6]

To explain interactive protocols in a more general setting, let us return for a moment to the class NP. A problem is in NP if it can be solved in polynomial time with the help of a magic coin. As explained in Chapter 4, this is equivalent to saying that whenever the answer is 'Yes' there is a short (that is, polynomial sized) certificate to that effect. (Nothing is claimed here about 'No' inputs.) This characterization can be rephrased in terms of a game between a **prover** and a **verifier**. Alice, the prover, is all-powerful, and she is trying to convince Bob, the verifier, who has only ordinary polynomial-time computing power, that an input to the problem at hand is a 'Yes' input.

For illustration, let us take a specific problem in NP; say, coloring a network of points and lines with three colors. Alice wants to convince Bob that the particular input network G is 3-colorable. Recall that no two neighboring points — points connected by a line — may be monochromatic. Since the problem is NP-complete, no-one knows of a polynomial-time algorithm for solving it, so that Bob, having only polynomial-time computing power, has no way of verifying Alice's claim on his own. He needs her to supply a proof. This she can do easily, by simply sending him a 3-coloring of G (see, for example, Fig. 4.4), which is really just the short 'Yes' certificate. Even with his limited power, Bob can then verify that the coloring is legal. Obviously, this kind of proof will never cause Bob to wrongly believe that Alice can 3-color G if she really can't.

---

[6] M. Blum (1983). 'How to Exchange (Secret) Keys', *ACM Trans. Comput. Syst.* **1**, 175–93.

Thus, we may say that a decision problem P is in NP if, whenever an input is a 'Yes' input, Alice can convince Bob of that fact in polynomial time, but if it is a 'No' input then neither Alice nor any other prover can convince Bob otherwise.

This little proving game is quite simple, and it requires a single round only: Alice sends the polynomially sized certificate to Bob, who promptly verifies that it is indeed a certificate.

There is a nice generalization of the prover/verifier concept that leads to a stronger notion of proof, the power of which we shall illustrate in the next section. The idea is to turn the process into an interactive one, with many rounds, and to allow the verifier to flip coins and ask the prover questions, all in polynomial time. The coin flipping helps Bob ask Alice random questions that she has no way of predicting. (Bob can hide his coin flips from Alice.) Thus, Alice remains all-powerful, but Bob now has the power to compute *probabilistically* in polynomial time. Moreover, the very notion of proving is also probabilistic: we no longer require an absolute proof, but only that Alice convince Bob of the 'Yes'-ness of an input with overwhelmingly high probability, in the sense of Chapter 5. We do allow mistakes (concluding that a 'No' input is really a 'Yes' input), but only with negligibly low probability.[7]

It is worth pausing to assess the philosophical significance of this notion. The one-round proving game associated with NP is very much like the standard way of proving a statement to someone in writing, say, as part of a lecture or a published article in mathematics: you supply what you claim is a complete proof, using all

---

[7] S. Goldwasser, S. Micali, and C. Rackoff (1989). 'The Knowledge Complexity of Interactive Proof Systems', *SIAM J. Comp.* **18**, 186–208.

the ingenuity you can muster, and I — the student in the lecture or the reader of the article — then check it as thoroughly as I can, to see whether I believe it or not. This is the normal 'you prove I check' way of proving things. In contrast, an **interactive proof** is a powerful, yet very natural, extension, more akin to the way mathematicians prove statements to each other orally: you supply some information, and I might then ask you questions, often tough ones you couldn't have predicted; you then supply answers and more information, and I continue to pester you with questions; and so on. This continues until I become convinced — in the probabilistic sense of the word, that is, with as high probability as I want (since we go on with this until *I* am happy) — that you are right, and then we stop. Of course, we require that the entire procedure take only a polynomial amount of time.

The really nice thing about interactive proofs is that in many cases they can be carried out without giving away any crucial information. So Alice can convince Bob of the 'Yes'-ness of an input without giving away the reasons for the 'Yes'-ness. Let us take a closer look at this additional possibility and its uses.

zero-knowledge proofs

Suppose I want to convince you that I know a certain secret. Say I claim to know what color socks the President of the United States is wearing at this very moment. Obviously, you don't believe me, and want a proof, right? The natural proof procedure that comes to mind is this: I tell you what color I claim they are, and we then immediately invite the President (who must be waiting outside) into the room to exhibit his socks, thus either refuting or verifying my claim. This protocol sounds fine. On the assumption that there were no microphones or moles in the room, you come away believing that I was right all along. You started out thinking I was lying — I simply *couldn't* have known this fact — and you end up convinced you were mistaken and that I indeed knew. (Let's also agree here that my chances of simply succeeding by a lucky guess are very slim, due to the large number of possible colors.) There is one problem, however. At the end of the day, when all is said and done, not only are you convinced that I wasn't lying and that I did indeed know the secret, but now you know the secret itself too! But perhaps I don't *want* you to. Maybe I don't even want you to know whether the President's socks are light or dark, or are a warm or a cool color. When the game is over, I want you to have no knowledge whatsoever of the secret itself; I would like you to come away with only the firm conviction that *I* know it, and nothing more.

This sounds absurd: how can I convince you that I know something without telling you that very something and having you verify it? Why on earth should you believe me about knowing something that is very hard to know (is there any reader out there who could have indeed found out, within minutes of being asked, what color the President's socks are?), if you yourself are not even allowed to see that something too and check for yourself?

Presidents and socks aside, the issue in question is to devise a method for Alice to prove to Bob the 'Yes'-ness of an input to some algorithmic problem, but without giving Bob any information about the reasons the input is a 'Yes' one. And we want to do this with an algorithmic problem for which Bob can't easily find out the 'Yes'-ness for himself. Returning to the 3-colorability of a network G as our example, we want Alice to be able to prove to Bob that she can color G with three colors, but we don't want Bob to get to know anything about the coloring itself. That is, not anything he couldn't have found out on his own. At the end of the proof we want Bob to know with overwhelming confidence that Alice wasn't lying. But we also want that to be the only new inform-ation he will have gained from the process. In particular, he will not be able to color G himself (in polynomial time), or even to repeat Alice's proof to someone else! Such seemingly paradoxical protocols are termed **zero-knowledge** (for obvious reasons).

We are making essential use of bad news here. In the socks example, you had no choice but to disbelieve me, since, although not a very interesting secret, the color of the President's socks is a secret indeed, and not something you can easily discover by making a couple of well-placed phone calls. In the same way, the fact that figuring out whether a network is 3-colorable is NP-complete renders Alice's claim a real secret: Bob cannot simply say 'big deal, I can find that out for myself'. He *can't* find it out, since he doesn't have more than a polynomial amount of time available for work, and no-one knows how to determine unaided whether Alice is a liar or not in an unacceptable amount of time. It is for this reason that Bob must start out assuming she does *not* know how to 3-color the network, and Alice must prove it to him.

Before showing how this can be done, it is worth remarking that zero-knowledge protocols have many applications in cryptography and secure communication. For example, we might want to devise smartcards to screen people entering a sensitive establishment (say, the headquarters of some top-secret intelligence agency), but we don't always want the establishment's personnel to know the identity of the people admitted, only that they were rightfully admitted. Or suppose a group of people want to set up a joint bank account. They would like to be able to withdraw and transfer money electronically, and would like the bank to enforce certain rules regarding who can withdraw money and how much can be withdrawn. But suppose they also want to prevent any bank employee from knowing exactly who withdraws; he or she may only know that the money was withdrawn legally, according to the rules. Such cases call for the ability to convince a verifier that you know some secret, some key or code (e.g. your legal entry id), but without divulging the secret itself, only the fact that you know it.

i can 3-color a network

Here then is a zero-knowledge protocol for coloring a network with three colors.[8] It is described here as if it takes place between two people, but it can be turned into a full-fledged algorithmic protocol, suitable for electronic applications. Also, we use a 10-point network for illustration, but if you had a powerful computer with you, we would have simply used a larger network, say, with 200 points, and its 3-colorability would have then really been beyond discovery.[9]

Alice shows Bob a network (see Fig. 6.3), and claims that it can be colored with three colors. Bob, in the polynomial time available to him, cannot verify that fact on his own, since the problem is NP-complete, so Alice attempts to prove it to him. She takes the network away, and secretly colors it with three colors, say, yellow,

---

[8] O. Goldreich, S. Micali, and A. Wigderson (1991). 'Proofs that yield nothing but their validity or all languages in NP have zero-knowledge proof systems', *J. Assoc. Comput. Mach.* **38**, 691–729.

[9] It is easy for Alice to prepare such a network. Just lay out 200 points, color them at random with three colors, and then in some fashion, randomly if you want, connect some of the points having different colors by lines.

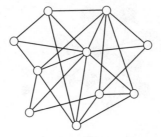

Fig. 6.3. A network.

red, and blue. She then carefully covers the colored points with small coins, and places the network in Bob's view (see Fig. 6.4(a)). She also tells Bob what colors she has used.[10] Bob is, of course, skeptical, but despite the fact that Alice is interested in eliminating his skepticism, she is not willing to expose the coloring. In fact, she is not willing to expose even a single pair of points not connected by a line, since whether these are colored with the same color or with different ones is part of her coloring strategy, about which she wants to give absolutely nothing away. Instead, she tells Bob that she is willing to expose any pair of *neighboring* points, that is, ones connected by a line. So Bob chooses a line in the network, at random if he wishes, and Alice removes the coins from the points at its end (see Fig. 6.4(b)). Bob then verifies that these two points are colored with different colors, as they should, and that the two colors are from among the three Alice listed. Clearly, if the exposed points violate one of these properties — she used, say, green, or

---

[10] When this protocol is carried out electronically, the secret coloring and covering, and all the stages that follow, are carried out using appropriate encoding and decoding, so that no cheating is possible.

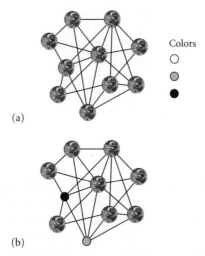

Colors
○
◐
●

(a)

(b)

Fig. 6.4. Covering a 3-colored network and exposing two neighbors.

has colored both the points red — Bob has shown that the coloring is not legal, thus shattering Alice's proof. However, if indeed the two colors are different, and they are from among the three Alice listed, he can't complain, but neither is he sure yet that the entire network is colored legally.

What now?

Rather than agreeing to expose more points, Alice takes back the coin-covered network, recolors it — this time using, say, brown, black, and white — and covers the new colors with the coins. She again tells Bob which colors she used, and again shows him the network. He again chooses a line in the network, and Alice promptly uncovers the two points at its ends. Again, Bob sees different colors, and they are indeed from among the three she said she had used. Once again he hasn't been able to refute Alice's claim.

This procedure is carried out repeatedly, as many times as Bob wants, until he is happy.

Why should Bob ever become really happy? Let's look at things from his point of view. The example network of Fig. 6.3 contains 23 connecting lines. After Alice passed the first test, meaning that Bob couldn't refute her claim from what he exposed, he is still far from being sure that Alice can 3-color the entire network. But he did have a chance of 1 in 23 of catching her lying if indeed she *cannot* color it. The reason for this is that Bob himself got to choose the pair of neighboring points that Alice was obliged to expose, and she had no idea ahead of time which pair he would choose. In fact, if Alice is indeed lying, and she *cannot* color the network, she knows that with this initial probe Bob has a chance of at least 1 in 23 of exposing her as a liar, since she must have either used a fourth color or colored two neighboring points the same. If we assume for the sake of the argument that Bob starts out with complete skepticism, that is, he is 100% sure (confident with probability 1) that she really *can't* 3-color the network, this confidence now goes down to $\frac{22}{23}$, which is less than 96%. This is the situation at the end of the first probe, or round.

Turning now to the second probe, from Alice's point of view this one was completely independent of the first one, and, as we know, independent probabilities are multiplied. Thus, the probability that Alice could pass the first *two* tests without really knowing how to 3-color the network is $\frac{22}{23} \times \frac{22}{23}$, or $(\frac{22}{23})^2$, which also represents Bob's new, lower, confidence in the fact that she is lying. This is about 91.5%. After a third test, his belief in her lying goes down to $(\frac{22}{23})^3$, which is 87.5%, and so on. As the process continues and the number of successful tests increases, this confidence decreases through increasingly larger powers of $\frac{22}{23}$, thus rapidly — exponentially, in fact — approaching 0.

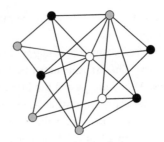

Fig. 6.5. A legal 3-coloring of the network of Fig. 6.3.

Bob can therefore stop the process whenever he is satisfied, and he will then be overwhelmingly convinced that Alice can 3-color the network (and in our example he is right; see Fig. 6.5), since he himself sets the level of confidence he wants.

In the general case of a network with N connecting lines, the probability goes down through powers of $(N–1)/N$. This is an exponential decrease, so that in practice you don't need too many rounds for the possibility to get really, really low, and several thousand rounds can still be carried out extremely fast by a smartcard interacting with a host computer.[11]

What about Bob's knowledge? What wisdom has he gained by going through this interactive proof protocol? Well, since he sees a different set of colors each time around, and since Alice doesn't indicate the correspondence between the color sets in the various tests, Bob has no knowledge of the color relationships between any

---

[11] Zero-knowledge protocols based on other NP-complete problems have an even faster decrease in probability. Many have a decrease rate that does not depend on N. If the decrease is 50% in each round, a game of 100 rounds brings Bob's belief in the fact that Alice is lying down to the negligibly small $1/2^{100}$.

points in the network, except to have seen several isolated pairs of neighboring points colored with different colors, as they should be. Such fragmented knowledge is of no help to him at all, since the colors used are changed around each time.[12] This argument can be formalized to show that Bob gains absolutely nothing — a zero amount of knowledge — about Alice's coloring scheme. Technically, this means that there is nothing he can find out in polynomial time now, after going through the entire proof protocol, that he couldn't have found out in polynomial time before he started probing Alice. In particular, as mentioned earlier, he can't even prove to someone else that the network can be 3-colored, although he himself is fully convinced! So Alice hasn't provided him with anything new, except what she had planned to, which was to convince him that she could 3-color the network.

This is a zero-knowledge protocol par excellence, and is once again an extremely interesting case of utilizing both the good and the bad news that algorithmics has to offer, in a powerful and crucial way. And again, we must remark that just like in public-key cryptography, where the conjectured-to-be-intractable problem of factoring is used as the hard problem, no-one knows whether a *provably* intractable problem can serve as the basis for zero-knowledge interaction. As of now, NP-complete problems are usually used for this. If P is ever shown to be equal to NP — that is, if the NP-complete problems are shown to have good solutions — all this will collapse; 3-coloring a network will then no longer be a difficult-to-discover secret.

---

[12] Actually, Alice can use the same three colors each time, but permuted, so that given any two tests Bob never knows the actual correspondence between the colors.

on millionaires, ballots, and more

Here are a couple of additional cases for which interactive protocols have been found.

Suppose a group of millionaires want to find out who is the richest, but they don't want to divulge any actual numbers about their own personal wealth. A protocol can be carried out that will result in everyone knowing who is the richest, but without giving away any further information. As explained earlier, giving away no further information means that no-one can find out anything about anyone else's wealth in polynomial time *after* the protocol is carried out, that he or she couldn't have found out in polynomial time beforehand. This includes absolute knowledge about one person's riches, or relative knowledge such as whether Joan is richer than Joe. Of course, knowledge that *follows* in polynomial time from the exposed information, such as the fact that everyone else has less money than the richest one, they do know.[13]

A similar protocol exists for managing secret votes, ballots, or elections. The way an anonymous electronic vote is usually carried out in a voting body, such as a parliament or a house of representatives, is by each voter pressing a 'Yes'/'No' button. This is fine, and if so desired the only results the voters will get to see are the general statistics and not the votes by name. The problem is that there will always be *someone* who can quite easily find out what the individual votes were (the software or hardware experts running the voting system, for example). Here too, recently developed

---

[13] A. C. Yao (1986). 'How to Generate and Exchange Secrets', *Proc. 27th IEEE Symp. Found. Comput. Sci.*, pp. 162–7.

computerized protocols make it possible to run a voting operation so that no information about individual votes is divulged to *anyone*, only the final desired count. In principle, such a protocol could also be carried out in a large nationwide election, and this could turn out to be the way things will be done in the future.

These two examples are special cases of a more general situation, whereby we are interested in computing some function F applied to N values. In the first example, the values represent the N millionaires' individual worth and the function F points to the maximum value (that is, it says which of the N values is largest). Had we wanted to compute the millionaires' average fortune, F would have provided that and nothing else. In the second example, the values are the individual 'Yes'/'No' votes of the N voters and the function F is the majority function, producing a grand 'Yes!!' or 'No!!' depending on which of the two values appears more often. Researchers have managed to devise a general interactive protocol that computes F in polynomial-time, and gives away *nothing* besides the value of F itself, and this for *any* function F in PTIME, i.e. one that is itself computable in the conventional way in polynomial-time. As usual, when it comes to intractable functions F, we know how to do this only with conjectured-to-be-intractable problems, such as factoring or certain NP-complete problems, but not provably intractable ones. Even so, the general technique is quite remarkable, and has many more potential applications.[14]

* * *

[14] O. Goldreich, S. Micali, and A. Wigderson (1987). 'How to Play Any Mental Game — A Completeness Theorem for Protocols with Honest Majority', *Proc. 19th ACM Symp. on Theory of Computing*, pp. 218–29.

Public-key cryptosystems, zero-knowledge interactive proofs, and many other ideas in this area, all exploit the bad news we have been discussing in this book in a most novel way. Still, they seem to leave us with mixed feelings, since no-one has been able to place the protocols involved on truly firm ground: their validity and security rests on news that we *think* is bad but don't know for sure.

If it weren't such serious business, the situation would be almost laughable: we find ourselves *hoping* that the news will stay bad!

chapter 7

can we ourselves
do any better?

Our treatment of the 'hard-core' bad news inherent in computing was actually completed at the end of Chapter 5, and the story we have set out to tell could have ended there. Chapter 6 was concerned with the questions of whether, when, and how things can be turned around, and we could have stopped there too. Nevertheless, it seems appropriate to end the book with bad news of a different kind, taking a brief look at some of the difficulties that arise when we think of computers as potentially intelligent.

One type of brain scanning technology has a computer analyzing, in real time, an enormous amount of data generated by numerous X-ray images of a human patient's brain, taken from increasing angles. The analyzed data is then used to automatically generate a cross-cut picture of the brain, providing information on tissue structure, and enabling identification of tumors or excess fluids. In striking contrast, no currently available computer can analyze a single, ordinary picture of the very same patient's face and determine the patient's age with an error margin of, say, five years, which most humans can.

Computers are able to control extremely sophisticated industrial robots that construct entire automobiles from their numerous parts. In contrast, today's most advanced computers are incapable of directing a robot to somehow organize my rather cluttered office (a task an average human could carry out easily — if hard-pressed, of course), or to construct a bird's nest from a pile of twigs (a feat an average bird can perform).

AI, or **artificial intelligence**, as it is called,[1] is a fascinating and exciting area of research. It is also controversial and speculative. Since it too involves computers running programs, AI is clearly susceptible to all the bad news we have already discussed. However, it suffers also from bad news of a 'softer' nature, which stems from the difficulty of characterizing true intelligence and figuring out how to emulate it.

The question of whether computers can think, someone once said, is just like the question of whether submarines can swim.[2] This analogy is quite apt. We all know more or less what sub-marines are capable of — and indeed they *can* do things that are akin to swimming — but 'real' swimming is something we associ-ate with entities of organic nature, such as humans and fish, not with submarines. In analogy, while we might have a pretty good idea of the capabilities of computational devices, real thinking is associated in our minds with *homo sapiens,* and perhaps also with some advanced mammals like apes and dolphins, but not with silicon-based collections of bits and bytes. Be this as it may, it is not *a priori* out of the question that we *could* mimic human intel-ligence with computers. But it's certainly not that simple.

---

[1] The term is due to J. McCarthy.

[2] This is due to E. W. Dijkstra.

algorithmic intelligence?

So how can a computerized robot put together a car? Why a car, but not a bird's nest? Why a CAT-scanner, but not a reliable face recognition system? What is so hard about building a computer that can be wheeled into my office on a platform, equipped with a battery of sophisticated video cameras, advanced robotic arms, and state-of-the-art software for a brain, that can take a good look around (emitting a 'tsk, tsk, David'), and can then efficiently figure out what is what, sort out and organize papers, books, files, and letters, store stationery and desktop items in the appropriate drawers, clean up coffee mugs and litter, dust, sweep, and shake out the rug, and leave a nice note saying 'your cleaning person for today has been R2D6'?

Well, there is no contradiction. In automobile manufacture, robots are programmed to carry out long and intricate sequences of operations by carefully prepared recipes, finding components in carefully predefined locations and doing carefully predefined things with them. Sometimes they can be reprogrammed to carry out different tasks, and some state-of-the-art ones are able to adapt their behavior somewhat to accommodate limited changing situations. But, in general, computerized robots are not able to take a look at new surroundings, comprehend and assess the situation, decide what has to be done, and then make a plan and execute it to completion. Brain tomography is carried out with the aid of complex, but well-defined, algorithmic procedures, whereas the ability to deduce a person's age from a photograph requires real intelligence.

There have been some successes — spectacular, when you know how hard it really is — in dealing with limited and carefully defined situations, such as telling different models of cars apart in pictures taken from new angles, or in a 'blocks world' in which a computer responds to things like 'place a red cube on top of two green cylinders and the yellow block'.[3] But we don't know how to deal with a pile of twigs of all shapes and sizes, or with a highly heterogeneous environment, like an office. Dealing with these requires levels of intelligence that are far, far beyond present-day algorithmic capabilities. Even the ability to take in a simple scene like a normal living room and 'understand' it, something every child can do, is far beyond the current capabilities of visualization systems.

Computerizing intelligence, making it algorithmic, is something we know far too little about. The very phrase 'artificial intelligence' — or, to rename it to fit in with the rest of the book, **algorithmic intelligence** — seems to be a contradiction in terms. We tend to view intelligence as our quintessential *non*programmable, and hence nonalgorithmic, characteristic. To many people the very idea of an intelligent machine doesn't sound quite right.

the Turing test

Many arguments have been put forward to render unthinkable the concept of an intelligent thinking machine. To think, some say, necessarily involves emotions and feelings, and no computer can hate, love, or become angry. Others claim that thinking intelligently necessarily entails originality and consciousness, and no computer can originate anything unless programmed ahead of time to do so, in which case it is no longer original. And we haven't even *tried* to deal with true consciousness yet. There are counter-

---

[3] T. Winograd (1972). *Understanding Natural Language.* Academic Press, New York.

arguments to many of these claims, but they are outside the scope of this book.[4] What can be said, though, is that a machine claimed to be intelligent must, at the very least, be able to exhibit human-like intelligent behavior. For this we do not require it to walk, see or talk like a human, only to reason and respond like one. Furthermore, whatever the agreed-on criteria for intelligence turn out to be, *someone* ought to be able to check whether a candidate machine fulfills them. And who is qualified to carry out such a test if not a real, intelligent human being? This leads to the idea that a machine ought to be labeled intelligent if it can convince an average human being that in terms of its intellect it is no different from another average human being.

Exactly fifty years ago Alan Turing proposed a way to set up such an experiment, now commonly called the **Turing test**.[5] The test takes place in three rooms. In the first there is a human interrogator (call her Alice), in the next there is another human, and in the third the candidate computer. The interrogator Alice knows the other two only by the names Bob and Carol, but doesn't know

[4] See J. R. Lucas (1961). 'Minds, Machines, and Gödel', *Philosophy* **36**, 112–17; H. Dreyfus (1979). *What Computers Can't Do* (rev. edn). Harper & Row, New York; Y. Wilks (1976). 'Dreyfus's Disproofs', *British J. Philos. Sci.* **27**, 177–85; D. R. Hofstadter (1979). *Gödel, Escher, Bach: An Eternal Golden Braid*. Basic Books, New York; H. Gardner (1985). *The Mind's New Science*. Basic Books, New York; J. V. Grabiner (1986). 'Computers and the Nature of Man: A Historian's Perspective on Controversies about Artificial Intelligence', *Bull. Amer. Math. Soc.* **15**, 113–126; R. Penrose (1990). *The Emperor's New Mind: Concerning Computers, Minds, & the Laws of Physics*. Viking Penguin, New York; J. R. Searle (1984). *Minds, Brains, and Science*. Harvard University Press, Cambridge, MA.

[5] A. M. Turing (1950). 'Computing Machinery and Intelligence', *Mind* **59**, 433–60.

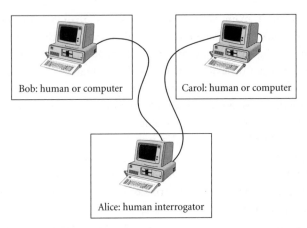

Fig. 7.1. The Turing test.

which is the human and which is the computer. The three rooms are equipped with computer terminals, with Alice's being connected to those of Bob and Carol (see Fig. 7.1). Now, Alice is given some fixed amount of time, say, 30 minutes, in which she must determine the correct identities of Bob and Carol. She is free to address any questions or statements whatsoever to either of them, and the computer has to make its best effort to deceive Alice, giving the impression of being human. The computer is said to pass the test if after the allotted time Alice doesn't know which of Bob or Carol is really the computer. In order to downplay the effect of a simple guess on Alice's part, the computer is actually required to pass several one-session tests, perhaps with different interrogators.[6]

---

[6] The programmed computer must be able to converse freely in a natural language such as English, but we waive the need for it to hear and talk; hence the electronic links.

Before proceeding, we should make it clear that no computer has ever come even marginally close to passing this test, and many researchers believe that none ever will.

Let us try to get a feel for the immense difficulty involved. Consider how an intelligent program would have to react to the following questions by Alice:

1. Are you a computer?

2. What is the time?

3. When was President Kennedy assassinated?

4. What is 454 866 296 × 66 407?

5. Can White win in less than four moves from the following chess position: ...?

6. Describe your parents.

7. How does the following poem strike you: ...?

8. What do you think of Charles Dickens?

9. What do you think of the upkeep cost for NATO, in view of the fact that millions of people around the globe are suffering from starvation?

The first two questions are rather easy for a computer to deal with. It should say 'No' when asked Question 1, and for Question 2 it can use the computer's built-in clock. Question 3 requires the program to be able to access a large pool of knowledge, comparable to the knowledge of a human being. That is fine, but the program's designer will just have to decide which items to include; simply giving it access to the *World Almanac* and the entire *Encyclopedia Britannica*, even in their electronic hyperlinked guises, won't do, for many reasons (one of which is that the sheer quantity of knowledge the computer might exhibit could easily give away its identity). Question 4 looks easy — computers seem to be best at this kind of feat — but it is also quite subtle: we might want to program the computer to wait a while before answering, because lightning speed will also give it away. Question 5, of course, requires it to have some knowledge of chess, including the ability to reason about a new position. But, then again, should we teach it checkers, Go, poker and bridge too? As to Question 6, although answers to such questions could be prepared in advance, Alice might respond to an answer by pursuing a certain unexpected detail that just wasn't provided with a ready-made answer (e.g. 'why exactly did your father decide to grow a beard?'). Questions 7, 8, and 9 are far more difficult. They require exhibiting preferences, opinions, feelings and the results of upbringing, together with an ability to explain the underpinnings of these and relate them to others. In short, the computer under scrutiny must be endowed with a real personality.

Hard stuff.

ELIZA and zupchoks

One of the difficulties in programming a computer to pass the Turing test is the great diversity of areas that the conversation can lead into. There has been some success in imitating human conversation in very limited areas of discourse. A program called ELIZA, written almost 35 years ago, was able to give an impressive performance as a psychoanalyst.[7] So impressive, in fact, that

---

[7] J. Weizenbaum (1966). 'ELIZA — A Computer Program for the Study of Natural Language Communication between Man and Machine', *Comm. Assoc. Comput. Mach.* **9**, 36–45.

people were known to actually 'confide' in it the way they would never confide in a fellow human! Here are a couple of typical exchanges:

Person: 'My wife says I am often depressed.'

ELIZA: 'I'm sorry to hear you are depressed.'

Person: 'The truth is I am quite unhappy.'

ELIZA: 'Do you think coming here will help you not to be unhappy?'

Person: 'Well, perhaps by talking to you I will find out why I hate my brother.'

ELIZA: 'Tell me more about your family.'

The interesting thing about ELIZA is the fact that it is not intelligent by any reasonable measure. It is actually quite dumb. In so far as it gives the impression of being a thoughtful therapist, it is really a shrewd cheat. Most often, it simply zeros in on a particular word or phrase it has been taught to look out for and responds by choosing, virtually at random, one of a small number of fixed responses. An excellent example of this is the response 'Tell me more about your family', triggered by the word 'brother'. Other times, ELIZA merely turns an incoming sentence into a question or a rather meaningless statement, as in the exchange concerning the person's unhappiness. To do all this, it utilizes a simple mechanism for figuring out the coarse structure of the input sentences.

Strange things happen when you really try to test ELIZA's intelligence, instead of just spurting forth your problems. In fact, if we said 'I was a sister in a monastery in Burma', or even 'I admired Sister Teresa', the program might very well respond with the same nonsensical 'Tell me more about your family'. Its response to the question about NATO is bound to be equally amusing. ELIZA, of course, has no chance of passing the Turing test. In fact, it was not intended to. The motivation behind ELIZA — and in this respect it was enormously successful — was to show that it is easy to *appear* intelligent; at least for a short while, to a sympathetic observer, and within a narrow domain of discourse. To be *really* intelligent is quite a different matter.

To further appreciate the difference between the genuine intelligence required to pass Turing's test, and the shallow, yet deviously deceptive conversational abilities of programs such as ELIZA, here is a hypothetical exchange between the Turing test interrogator Alice and a really intelligent candidate, say Bob:[8]

Alice: 'What is a zupchok?'

Bob: 'I have no idea.'

Alice: 'A zupchok is a flying, novel-writing whale. It has been carefully cultivated in a laboratory over several generations to ensure that its fins evolve into wing-like things that enable it to fly. It has also been gradually taught to read and write. It has a thorough knowledge of modern literature, and has the ability to write publishable mystery stories.'

Bob: 'How weird!'

Alice: 'Do you think zupchoks exist?'

Bob: 'No way. They cannot.'

Alice: 'Why?'

---

[8] Adapted from I. Pohl and A. Shaw (1981). *The Nature of Computation: An Introduction to Computer Science.* Computer Science Press, Rockville, MD.

Bob: 'For many reasons. First of all, our genetic engineering capabilities are far from adequate when it comes to turning fins into wings, not to mention our inability to cause 10-ton engineless creatures to defy gravity just by flapping those things. Secondly, the novel-writing part doesn't even deserve response, since producing a good story requires much more than the technical ability to read and write. The whole idea seems ridiculous. Don't you have anything more interesting to talk about?'

To carry out this conversation, Bob, be it human or computer, must display extremely sophisticated abilities. He (or it) must possess a large amount of **knowledge** on specific topics, such as whales, flying, novel-writing, and gravity. It must be able to **learn** about a totally new concept, taking in the definitions and relating them to what it already knows. And it must be able to **deduce** things from its newly acquired knowledge, such as the fact that genetic engineering is more relevant to zupchoks than, say, algebraic topology or Chinese philosophy. (In this particular case it must also have a sense of humor.) Indeed, knowledge, learning, and deduction are three fundamental areas of artificial intelligence research.

heuristics

Game playing is one of the specialized areas in which AI research has achieved significant results.[9] For example, there are many

---

[9] D. Michie (1995). 'Game Mastery and Intelligence', in *Machine Intelligence 14* (K. Furakawa, D. Michie, and S. Muggleton, eds.). Clarendon Press, Oxford.

programs that play checkers extremely well, routinely beating their designers. The best-known of these is an incredibly good program called Chinook.[10] The same goes for other games too. More than 20 years ago, for example, a computer program was already able to beat the world champion in backgammon. (This did not make the program the new champion, as the game was not played in an official tournament, but the win was a win nevertheless.) These days, a program called TD-Gammon routinely plays on the level of the world's top backgammon players.

As to computerized chess, this is a topic with a remarkable history, involving amazingly sophisticated software, first-line human players, prize-carrying challenges, public matches, and triumphs and frustrations on both sides. The main computerized players included programs with names like Chess Genius, Zugzwang, StarSocrates, and Deep Thought, and the most formidable kid on the block: Deep Blue.[11] The bottom line is this: in May 1997, Gary Kasparov, world chess champion and one of the best chess players of all time, played against Deep Blue, a program written by a group of IBMers and running on a supercomputer. The six-game match was won by Deep Blue, 3.5 to 2.5.[12] Though somehow expected, this victory stunned the world. To many people it is obvious that a computer program will eventually

[10] J. Schaeffer (1997). *One Jump Ahead: Challenging Human Supremacy in Checkers.* Springer-Verlag, New York.

[11] D. Levy and M. Newborn (1991). *How Computers Play Chess.* Computer Science Press, New York; M. Newborn and M. Newborn (1996). *Kasparov Versus Deep Blue: Computer Chess Comes of Age.* Springer-Verlag, New York.

[12] B. Pandolfini (1997). *Kasparov and Deep Blue: The Historic Chess Match Between Man and Machine.* Fireside, New York.

become the official world champion in chess. At present, the international federations still refuse to rate chess programs, and the US chess authorities have been very reluctant to have them compete in official activities. But these are technicalities, it seems. Sooner or later an official title will be bestowed upon Deep Blue or one of its descendants.

This does not mean that such programs are perfect. If they were, they would never lose a game. Why can't programs play *perfect* chess or checkers, and hence routinely and easily beat the very best human players? Why can't a computer run through all possible moves and always choose the best one? The answer lies in the number of possibilities. For some simple games there is no problem. In tic-tac-toe (noughts and crosses), the first player has nine possible moves, to which the opponent can respond in one of eight ways, to which the first player can respond in one of seven, and so on, all the way down to one last move. The total number of possibilities to check in an entire game is thus no more than 9!, or 362 880. This means that a computer can be easily programmed to play perfect tic-tac-toe.

With chess, on the other hand, the story is quite different. White has 20 possible first moves, and the average number of next moves from an arbitrary chess position is around 35. The number of moves in a game (twice the number of rounds) can easily reach 80 or 100. This means that the number of possibilities to check in a typical game might be something like 35^{100}. In Chapter 3 we saw some such numbers: 35^{100} is many, many, *many* orders of magnitude larger than the number of protons in the universe, or the number of microseconds or nanoseconds since whenever …. Even if we ignore the bookkeeping and memory space involved in a brute-force trip through all possible moves, and assume that each move can be tested in, say, a nanosecond, there is simply no way that computers can explicitly contemplate each and every possibility in any reasonable amount of time. So there is no hope for a perfect chess program. A world champion yes, but a perfect program no.[13]

How, then, do good chess programs operate? Well, this is too complex a topic to get into here, but — very briefly — one of their methods is to use **heuristics**, or rules of thumb. A typical heuristic search uses intuitive rules, incorporated into the program by the programmer, instructing it to ignore certain portions of the sea of possibilities. For example, one kind of rule might prescribe that if during the last four moves nothing has changed within the two-square vicinity of a certain pawn, that pawn will not be moved, and the search can ignore all possibilities that follow from moving it. This rule might turn out to be very insightful — it definitely results in less work on the part of the program — but, of course, it could cost us the game; Kasparov might have advanced that very pawn to win the game in five moves. Obviously, this is a very simple-minded example, and the heuristics embodied in real chess-playing programs are far more sophisticated. They are heuristics nevertheless, and a program guided by them can very well miss the best move.

A nice way to explain the nature of heuristic search is to consider what happens when you lose a contact lens. You could carry out a *blind* search, by bending over and feeling around for the lens at random. You could carry out a *systematic* search, by methodically searching ever-larger circles around a central starting point. This search is bound to succeed eventually, but it might be very time-

---

[13] The numbers for checkers are not quite as large, but perfect checkers is also out of the question.

consuming. A third possibility is *analytic* search, whereby the precise mathematical equations governing the fall of the lens are formulated and solved, taking into account wind, gravity, and air friction, as well as the precise topography, tension, and texture of the surface. This too, if carried out correctly, is guaranteed to succeed, but for obvious reasons is impractical.

In contrast to these methods, most of us would use a *heuristic* search. We would first identify the approximate direction of the fall and make an educated guess as to the distance the lens could have gone by falling; we would then limit the search to the resulting area. Still, heuristics cannot guarantee success; after all, rules of thumb are only rules of thumb. (There is, of course, a fifth approach, the *lazy* search, which calls for searching for the closest optician and purchasing a new lens.)

In a sense, using heuristics is like tossing coins. In Chapter 5 we saw how things can be improved by following the whims of randomness; the set of possibilities we thought we had to search through is significantly reduced, and many are left unexplored. We were thus willing to label a number 'prime' although we hadn't checked every possible witness to its non-primality. Since success is not guaranteed there either, it is tempting to view coin tossing as a *blind* heuristic, a sort of intuitionless rule of thumb. But there is a major difference. With probabilistic algorithms, analysis replaces intuition. By considering carefully defined sets of ignorable possibilities, and using randomization to decide which to actually ignore, we are able to analyze the probability of success rigorously, making precise statements about the algorithm's performance. This is often not true for algorithms that use heuristics.

This account of heuristics is overly simplistic. In actuality there is much more going on than a few simple rules that cause the program to ignore some of the possibilities in a search. There has to be a way to *evaluate* the quality of such situations in the search. For example, the designers of chess-playing algorithms must deal with the issue of what is the 'value' to White of a given board configuration. The problem of evaluating situations to help the algorithm reach a decision is one of the main challenges of heuristic programming.

In a medical diagnosis system the number of possibilities is also enormous, and a heuristic search must take place, with the patient's observable symptoms and his or her answers to queries driving the system's navigation among the directions and possibilities. The evaluation problem here, which determines how relevant a particular set of possibilities is to the sought-after final diagnosis, is incredibly difficult. Indeed, one of the most useful outcomes of research in AI has been the development of sophisticated evaluation techniques for heuristic search.

what is knowledge?

Heuristics and heuristic search constitute just one aspect of algorithmic intelligence. We also have to find ways to represent the **knowledge** that intelligent algorithms manipulate. The what-to-do-next parts of many AI programs are special, being based upon the 'soft' notion of heuristics, rather than on the 'harder', deterministic, analysis-driven basis of conventional algorithmics. In analogy, many of the what-are-we-talking-about parts of AI programs are also special, being based upon the 'soft' notion of associative knowledge and erratically connected data, rather than on the well-organized, carefully regulated data structures and data bases of conventional algorithmics.

So what *is* knowledge?

That twice four is eight and that France is in Europe is knowledge, but so is the fact that all giraffes have long necks, that Isaac Newton was brilliant, and that academics who do not publish perish. But what is 'long' and what is 'brilliant', and is 'perish' to be taken literally? How do we represent such facts in our minds or in our computer's knowledge bases, and how do we use them? No program can be labeled intelligent — be it one that operates in a narrow domain, such as chess or a blocks world, or a general-purpose candidate for passing the Turing test — unless it has an appropriate mechanism for storing, retrieving, and manipulating knowledge.

The difficulty is rooted in the observation that human knowledge does not consist merely of a large collection of facts. It is not only the sheer number and volume of the facts that is overwhelming (some researchers estimate the number at 30–50 million), but, to a much larger extent, their interrelationships and dynamics. Items of knowledge are intertwined in the most intricate and complex ways, having numerous components, attributes, and levels of abstraction. And they constantly change, grow, and shift, as do the interconnections. We know very little about the way we ourselves store and manipulate the immense quantities of knowledge accumulated over our lifetime. It is easy to say that we too are but finite machines, and are therefore amenable to simulation. The fact of the matter is that a human's knowledge base is *incredibly* complex, and works in ways that are still far beyond our comprehension.

Still, impressive advances have been made in computerized knowledge representation, and many models have been suggested for use by intelligent programs. Some of these are based on standard kinds of database systems, and others on carefully constructed logical formalisms. One of the most interesting proposals for this involves **neural nets**, a computational model that attempts to simulate the relationships and transfer of information between neurons in our brains. However, once outside a small well-defined domain of discourse, the relationships become far more intricate than we know how to model in this fashion, and current neural nets become vastly inadequate. Retrieving the knowledge items that are relevant to some decision that an intelligent program has to make is a truly formidable task. Neural nets have been used beneficially for many kinds of computerized jobs, taking advantage of their flexibility and ability to adapt, and thus learn (we shall be discussing learning shortly), but they too are far from exhibiting true intelligence.

Particular kinds of knowledge-intensive programs are called **expert systems**. These are based on rules that a human expert employs in solving a particular problem. A typical expert system is constructed by questioning the expert about the ways that he or she utilizes expertise in tackling the problem at hand. The (human) questioner, sometimes called a knowledge engineer, attempts to discover and formulate the rules used by the expert, and the expert system then uses these rules the guide to search for a solution to a given instance of the problem.

Expert systems with acceptable — often excellent — levels of performance have been constructed for carrying out some forms of medical diagnosis, for determining the structure of a molecule from its atomic formula and its mass spectrogram, for finding oil-rich areas, and for helping in the configuration of computer systems. We must realize, however, that in addition to relying on heuristic search, the rules that control the operation of an expert system are formed by questioning experts who might not always operate according to rigid rules. The chances of unexpected, perhaps catastrophic, behavior in an expert system are therefore non-negligible. Some people put it this way: in an emergency, would you be willing to be taken care of by a computerized intensive care unit that was programmed according to the expert system paradigm? Under a rare set of circumstances, the unit could administer the wrong medicine or shut a crucial valve at the wrong moment, since its behavior is governed by rules that reflect interviews with expert doctors who might not necessarily act in an unusual case according to well-formed rules that they are able to articulate.

The knowledge representation problem becomes particularly acute when we consider **learning** and **planning**. Consider the task of constructing a checkers program that learns from its mistakes. How can this be done? How do we represent the relevant data? Should the program simply make a list of the positions and moves that turned out to be bad in previous games, and then run through them each time to avoid repeating a mistake, or should it try to remember and update more general rules of good play, to be used for modifying its heuristics? These questions become all the more difficult when the subject area is wider: how do children learn? How do they represent the knowledge that enables them to recognize objects or to synthesize sentences? How do adults remember and retrieve the vast amount of knowledge that enables them to learn how to write an essay, how to organize personal finances, or how to adapt to a new environment?

The ability to plan is another intelligent skill. Some sophisticated mobile robots, operating within relatively simple surroundings, are capable of planning a sequence of movements that will take them to their destination. How do they do so? Do they simply carry out a search through all possibilities, or do they utilize more subtle knowledge that enables them to look ahead, so to speak, and really plan with the goal in mind? Again, broader domains make things much harder: how does a person plan a trip, outline a scheme for ending the year with a positive balance, or devise a strategy to win a war? Way too little is known about how we ourselves deal with these tasks, and as a result we are very far from being able to teach them to a computer, even with the aid of learning mechanisms such as neural nets.

understanding natural language

A nice way to better appreciate the difficulty of mechanizing intelligence is to look a little closer at the comprehension of ordinary natural language.

We shall concentrate here on *understanding* the language — not merely on recognizing the words — but it is instructive to first see what can happen when a speech-recognition program makes mistakes. The sentence

Her presence made all the difference

can be easily misunderstood and interpreted as

Her presents made all the difference

Similarly,

Any Japanese car responds well

can be heard as

Any Japanese corresponds well

and the well-known American statement

I pledge allegiance to the flag

when mumbled fast, as school-kids will, can be understood as

I led the pigeons to the flag

Speech-recognition programs are a pun lover's paradise.[14]

When it comes to semantics the subtleties are much greater. Many sentences can't be understood without the context, and without the special nuances, phrases, and slang of the language at hand. Sometimes it is also necessary to be familiar with the idiosyncrasies of the person speaking. A famous example involves the aphorism

The spirit is willing but the flesh is weak

As the story goes, this sentence was subjected first to a simple dictionary-based computer translation into Russian, followed by a similar translation back into English. The result was

The vodka is strong but the meat is rotten

Ambiguity is the main culprit. Consider the following:

Jim sat down at the table and found a large fruit salad on a plate next to the basket of bread. It took him a while, but he finally managed to eat and digest it all.

What did Jim eat? Was it the salad, the bread, or both? In some contexts it might be the plate or the basket; it could even be the table! Here grammar alone won't help much. The intended meaning, probably hinted at subtly by the context, is what counts.

---

[14] Hearing the pledge of allegiance as having to do with pigeons was described by W. Safire in one of his 'On Language' columns in *The New York Times* some years ago. See W. Safire (1980). *On Language*, Times Books.

The following sentences are grammatically identical but they differ in the relationships between their various parts:

The lost children were found by the searchers
The lost children were found by the mountain
The lost children were found by nightfall

Obviously, the correct interpretation depends on the meaning of the words 'searchers', 'mountain', and 'nightfall'. And these kinds of things are incredibly difficult to predict and computerize, given the vast number of words in English. The same phenomenon occurs in these sentences:

The thieves stole the jewels, and some of them were later sold
The thieves stole the jewels, and some of them were later caught
The thieves stole the jewels, and some of them were later found

In this case, the word 'sold' refers to the jewels, 'caught' refers to the thieves, and 'found' can refer to either. Actually, even that much is not obvious. It is possible that the story takes place in a country where thieves are sold as slaves, rendering the first sentence ambiguous too. If the second sentence had 'threw the jewels out of the window' instead of 'stole the jewels', it would also be ambiguous. Here again, semantics and understanding, and the issue of knowledge, appear in all their severity. We utilize an *enormous* amount of knowledge in disambiguating and understanding ordinary English, besides just the words and the grammar. Identifying that knowledge, and representing it in ways that capture its intricate interrelationships and enable useful retrieval, re-emerges as the central and most fundamental problem in computerizing natural language.

We are not saying that it is impossible or hopeless, just that it is far, *far* more difficult than it seems, and it involves far, far more than meets the eye.

To end this chapter, here are three hypothetical exchanges between a human being and a futuristic intelligent phone-answering machine, in, say, 25 years.[15] When reading them, it is worth putting amusement aside for a moment. Try to think of the way we humans would have dealt with the situations they raise, and of the hopelessness of programming a computer to deal with them intelligently.

Conversation 1

Machine: 'Hello, this is Jim's phone.'

Voice: 'Oh, it's you. Listen, this is his boss. I really need to get Jim right away. Can you locate him and have him call me?'

Machine: 'I'm sorry, Mr Hizboss, Jim is playing golf this afternoon and left orders not to be disturbed.'

Voice: 'He is, is he? Well, look, I'm thin on patience this afternoon. This is *his boss* calling, you idiot, not Mr Hizboss. Get Jim. Now!'

Machine: 'I'm pleased to hear that you are spending time with your patients this afternoon, Dr Thin. Business must be good. If you want to reach Jim's boss just dial 553-8861. Certainly you would never find him here in Jim's office; we have him listed in our directory under the alias of The Monster.'

Voice: 'Take this message, you son of a chip, and get it straight. Tell him he is not worth the spacebar on your keyboard. He is fired!'

(... *Click* ...)

---

[15] Adapted with permission from R. W. Lucky (1986). 'The Phone Surrogate', *IEEE Spectrum* **23**(5), 6.

Conversation 2

Machine: 'Hello, this is Jim's phone.'

Voice: 'Oh, hello, you darling machine. I just wanted to check that we're still on for dinner and whatever.'

Machine: 'Of course, Sue. I have you with him for Thursday at the usual spot.'

Voice: 'This is Jim's fiancée, Barbara. Who is Sue?'

Machine: 'Oh, Barbara, I didn't recognize your voice. I've never heard of anyone named Sue.'

Voice: 'But you just said he was meeting with Sue on Thursday.'

Machine: 'Oh, *that* Sue. Are you sure you have the right number? This is Martin Finch's phone.'

Voice: 'You can't pull that trick on me. Tell Jim it's all over!'

Machine: 'You have reached a nonworking number. Please check your listing and redial.'

(… *Click* …)

Conversation 3

Machine: 'Hello, this is Jim's phone.'

Voice: 'Are you satisfied with your present investments? Have you considered the advantages of tax-free municipal bonds? To hear more, please give your name and address after the beep.'

(… *Beep* …)

Machine: 'Err, … this is Jim's phone.'

Voice: 'Thank you Mr Jimzfone. Let me tell you more about our unusual investment opportunities …'

postramble

We have already said that computers are amazing. Bookstores and bookshelves are brimming with books that talk about what computers can do and how to get the most out of them. This is the good news, and this book concentrated on the bad.

Instead of summarizing the hard facts and the unknowns, it seems appropriate to close with another amusing story. This time an imaginary scene, in which four robots, built in four of the leading AI labs in the USA, are trying to use their intelligence to get across a busy highway.[1]

The first comes from a laboratory in which logical deduction and planning are crucial parts of its AI research. This robot stands by the side of the road, looking here and there, dizzied by the cars and trucks whizzing by, and waiting for the situation to stabilize so that it can use its deep and contemplative deduction abilities to devise a plan for crossing. This, of course, never happens.

The second robot is from a lab that excels in the complex robotics of mechanical propulsion: walking, rolling, and hopping. This one-legged Pogo-stick robot is in the midst of the traffic, frantically jumping up and down and to and fro, again and again barely

---

[1] This is based loosely on a folklore joke that is reproduced in
K. J. Hammond (1989). *Case-Based Planning: Viewing Planning as a Memory Task*. Academic Press, New York, pp. xxi–xxii.

avoiding being hit, but making no progress whatsoever towards the other side.

The third originates in a large and rich lab that does many different kinds of grand-scale AI research and manages to attract big grant money. The road is littered with the crushed remains of many of this lab's robots. Many more of these gallant and loyal robots are waiting on the side, to be sent out to try again, one after the other, just like infantry charging out of the trenches in World War I.

The fourth lab views the heart and soul of AI to be the comprehension, analysis, and synthesis of natural language. Its robot sits at the side of the road, nods slowly and says, 'Yes, I know; and that reminds me of another story …'.

index